Leadership, Myth, & Metaphor

Leadership, Myth, & Metaphor

Finding Common Ground to Guide Effective School Change

Daniel Cherry   Jeff Spiegel

Foreword by Michael Fullan

CORWIN PRESS
A SAGE Publications Company
Thousand Oaks, California

Portions of the ISLCC Standards are used throughout the book. They are reprinted with permission of the Council of Chief State School Officers (1996). *Interstate School Leaders Licensure Consortium (ISLLC) standards for school leaders.* Washington, DC: Author.

The Interstate School Leaders Licensure Consortium (ISLLC) Standards were developed by the Council of Chief State School Officers (CCSSO) and member states. Copies may be downloaded from the Council's Web site at www.ccsso.org.

For information:

 Corwin Press
A Sage Publications Company
2455 Teller Road
Thousand Oaks, California 91320
www.corwinpress.com

Sage Publications Ltd.
1 Oliver's Yard
55 City Road
London, EC1Y 1SP
United Kingdom

Sage Publications India Pvt. Ltd.
B-42, Panchsheel Enclave
Post Box 4109
New Delhi 110 017 India

Printed in the United States of America

Library of Congress Cataloging-in-Publication Data

Cherry, Daniel.
Leadership, myth, & metaphor : finding common ground to guide effective school change / Daniel Cherry, Jeff Spiegel.
     p. cm.
Includes bibliographical references and index.
ISBN 1-4129-2707-2 (cloth)—ISBN 1-4129-2708-0 (pbk.)
    1. Educational leadership. 2. Educational change. I. Title: Leadership, myth, & metaphor. II. Spiegel, Jeff. III. Title.
LB2805.C482 2006
371.2—dc22   2005022987

This book is printed on acid-free paper.

06   07   08   09   10   10   9   8   7   6   5   4   3   2   1

Acquisitions Editor:	Elizabeth Brenkus
Editorial Assistant:	Desirée Enayati
Production Editor:	Laureen A. Shea
Copy Editor:	Mary L. Tederstrom
Typesetter:	C&M Digitals (P) Ltd.
Proofreader:	Caryne Brown
Indexer:	Nara Wood
Cover Designer:	Rose Storey

Contents

Foreword

*L*eadership, Myth, & Metaphor is one of the most powerful books on metaphors available. Cherry and Spiegel give us three major evocative images: the Touchstone, the Advocate, and the Parent. Each corresponding section of the book has a rich array of images, inspiring directions, and reflective and action-oriented ideas.

What makes this book special is its focus on leadership in a way that allows each of us to find the image or combination of images on which to build our effectiveness. Leadership metaphors have the virtue of covering all the bases, from moral purpose through the ins and outs of organizational change.

This is a deeply human book, not only in its treatment of spiritual leadership in its own right but also in the many individual stories about actual leaders. We see leadership in action through the eyes of specific leaders in the situations they face. In addition to leaders that the authors have encountered in their own work, they also profile authors from the research literature, which lends further authority to the message.

The elements of this book that I find especially helpful are its themes, its reflective power, and its instruments and techniques for identifying and acting on one's own leadership potential. Cherry and Spiegel have written a book that can release us from limiting and negative images and provide a broad springboard for reaching new levels of accomplishment. The reader should take full advantage of what this energizing book has to offer.

—Michael Fullan, University of Toronto

Preface

The impetus for writing this book comes from our desire to share with readers the power of metaphor as a remarkable tool for leadership development and organizational change. With the shadow of No Child Left Behind looming over the landscape of America's schools, educational leaders have focused their attention on the issue of accountability at the expense of creative and successful approaches to school reform. From countless conversations with principals and superintendents we've learned how leaders struggle to fit the square peg of their core values and intrinsic beliefs into the round hole of mandated competencies and the continual shrill calls to "get back to basics." The result of this quagmire is often evidenced by leaders' loss of vision, confused sense of mission, and frustrated purpose.

Our book is about another kind of "back to basics" that offers hope for our schools and inspiration for those seeking to reconcile their personal and professional goals with the call for productive institutional change. Because this is a book about metaphoric reframing, the term "on fertile ground" seems to resonate with our message. It suggests for us how contemporary writers on school leadership planted the seeds and nurtured the soil upon which our ideas germinated and began to grow. We reflected on the literature and discovered a provocative tool for helping individuals and organizations think creatively and act proactively to address the challenges confronting them.

We've titled our book *Leadership, Myth, & Metaphor* because it demonstrates how metaphors often reveal unconscious beliefs that influence leadership behaviors. For the past three years, more than 250 superintendents and principals attended a professional development project funded by the Bill and Melinda Gates Foundation titled NHSALT (New Hampshire School Administrators Leading with Technology). During that period, extensive interviews explored administrators' core values and intrinsic beliefs through metaphor. One of the significant results of these meetings was that administrators not only identified an appropriate leadership metaphor for themselves, but were also motivated to apply reframing through metaphor to address organizational, pedagogical, and change issues that they were confronting in their schools. The successful use of metaphor at the organizational level confirmed for us its value as a meaningful tool that can be used systemically to move institutions to deeper levels of performance.

Our book identifies three leadership archetypes: the *Touchstone,* the *Advocate,* and the *Parent.* These exemplars characterize specific value orientations and administrative behaviors that leaders discussed by way of metaphor. Their reflections also addressed the need for practical and successful approaches to school reform and organizational change.

We realized it would seem whimsical if our work focused only on the spiritual archetypes of leaders. The real significance of this book resides in the final chapters, which discuss and demonstrate the uses of metaphor in the workplace. We've applied a developmental process that takes the reader from theoretical perspectives to real-world exemplars and finally back to the reader to integrate both theory and practice through a series of novel activities.

What follows is a progression of creation stories in the form of personal and institutional myths revealed by metaphor. We found a way to gain entry into the wisdom and compelling sense of purpose that inspire leaders to act on their intrinsic beliefs and move their organizations to higher quality performance, enhanced collective action, and proactive decision making and problem solving. Besides public and private school principals and superintendents, we believe this book is relevant to a broad spectrum of audiences, including college professors and campus leaders, business managers and corporate executives, organizers for philanthropic organizations, and professional association leaders. Our goal from the outset has been to bring any leader and institution from negative or self-limiting practices to more engaging, fulfilling, and effective work through metaphor.

Acknowledgments

We were particularly impressed that both women and men were comfortable in reframing metaphorically. We wish to thank the following principals and superintendents from Vermont, New Hampshire, and New York for their willingness to use metaphor to reflect on their work and to gain further insights about the values and beliefs that inspired their practice. Some of these administrators were compelled to provide personal essays, poems, works of art, artifacts, and metaphors about them created by their colleagues to describe more fully the influences on their work: Suzan Gannett, Tim Rice, Susan Dell, Norm Couture, Stan Shupe, David Michaud, Sherri Gregory, Jeni Mosca, Joanne Boddy, Gwen Mitchell, Dottie Frazier, Steven Beals, James Friel, Bob Braman, Robert McKenney, Pam Stiles, Amanda Lecaroz, Mark Vallone, Tony Silva, Marie Samaha, Carol Ann Finnegan, Ellie Emery, Richard Larcom, Mike Amsden, Rose Darrow, Tom Ferenc, Sue Blair, Joanne Patelle, Bill Gurney, Jeff Keene, Linda Brenneman, Nancy Andrew, Don Hart, Susan Finer, Deb Gillespie, Mike Cirre, Loretta Murphy, John Crist, Ellen Turcotte, Barbara Gendron, Kathy Hancock, Bob Sampson, Sue Whitbeck, Paul Couture, Norm Dellaire, Patrick Andrew, Barry Connell, Dennis Harrington, Jerry Benson, Peter Durso, Nicole Saginor, Shiela Moran, Ira Weston, and Cynthia Fowlkes.

Special recognition goes to Kathleen Laureti, Richard Jenisch, and Bryan Lane. As exemplars, their essays spoke volumes about the courage, dedication, and inspired focus characterizing the work of the three leadership archetypes featured in our book.

We also wish to acknowledge our appreciation to the NHSALT design team: Dr. Charles Mitsakos, Dr. Christy Hammer, Mary Heath, Rose Colby, Dr. Jane Legacy, Dr. Darrell Lockwood, and Peggy McAllister. Their support and vision for educational reform created opportunities for leaders to reflect on their work in new and provocative ways.

Finally, special thanks to Lizzie Brenkus, Acquisitions Editor, Corwin Press. The advice, critique, and encouragement we received from her defined her Touchstone, Advocate, and Parent qualities.

Corwin Press gratefully acknowledges the contributions of the following individuals:

Jennifer Baadsgaard, Assistant Principal
Roosevelt High School
San Antonio, TX

Karen Brinkman, Principal
Millikan High School
Long Beach, CA

Brenda Dietrich, Superintendent
Auburn-Washburn USD 437
Topeka, KS

Robert Fowls, Head of School
Trinity Lutheran School
Bend, OR

Teresa Miller, Associate Professor
College of Education, Kansas State University
Manhattan, KS

Rena Richtig, Professor
Central Michigan University
Mt. Pleasant, MI

About the Authors

Daniel Cherry is cofounder of Deconstructing the Box, a consulting group that specializes in leadership, organizational change, and technology. Most recently he was the director of the New Hampshire School Administrators Leading with Technology (NHSALT) program, funded through a grant from the Bill and Melinda Gates Foundation. Dan is also a member of the Association of Supervision and Curriculum Development (ASCD) faculty and has been recognized as an expert in improving instruction through the use of technology. As an educator, Dan has ten years' experience as a classroom teacher, seven years' experience as a technology director, and five years' experience working at the state level for the New Hampshire Department of Education. Dan has been recognized as a Distinguished Speaker at the Christa McAuliffe Technology Conference, and he has presented at many national education conferences. After hours, Dan spends time with his son Aaron, his daughter Danielle, and his wife Sandra. His hobbies include coaching Little League baseball and youth basketball, playing his string bass, singing in church, participating in community theatre, and cheering for the Buffalo Bills.

Jeff Spiegel is currently the assistant superintendent for the New Hampshire SAU 43 School District and cofounder of the consulting firm Deconstructing the Box. He was a Graduate Fellow at New York University's Institute for Developmental Studies and a Fulbright Memorial Scholar to Japan. Jeff earned his doctorate in educational leadership and policy studies at the Graduate College of the University of Vermont. His research focused on reframing female leaders' personal myths by way of metaphor. Jeff's career in education has evolved from classroom teacher in central Harlem to special educator and adjunct faculty member at Johnson State College and St. Michael's College in Vermont. For 18 years he served as an elementary school principal and organizational consultant in New Hampshire. He has written extensively and presented at numerous state and national conferences on topics addressing school culture development, differentiated instructional design, and creative problem solving for educational and organizational reform. Jeff has just completed two years as the New Hampshire principal in residence for the NHSALT project, funded by the Bill and Melinda Gates Foundation.

Introduction

The Spirit of Leadership

There is nothing more difficult to take in hand, more perilous to conduct, or more uncertain in its success, than to take the lead in the introduction of a new order of things, because the innovator has for enemies all those who have done well under the old conditions, and lukewarm defenders in those who may do well under the new.

—Machiavelli

When asked to consider a metaphor that best described her as a leader, the principal blushed slightly. "Hmm," she mused. "I'm not really a metaphoric thinker." Then, after a pause, she took a risk and likened herself to a peach pit. "I guess you could say I'm at the core of providing fertile knowledge," she offered tentatively. Feeling encouraged, she added, "The peach pit cultivates development much like what I try to do in providing vision. My job is to allow information and experience to grow around our mission to foster continuous growth." She sat back and smiled sheepishly, obviously pleased with her new perspective. "You know," she confessed, "I've never thought of myself like that. What a novel way to describe my sense of purpose."

This is a book that tells similar stories about leaders. It digs deeper into the spiritual myths that inspire their work. By accessing images and artifacts to describe their fundamental beliefs, we listened as principals used metaphors to analyze and reframe their professional mission. Often their stories created unique and refreshing views about their work and life ambitions. For them, metaphors were the "right way" out of the left brain to reveal deeper understandings about themselves.

The impetus for writing this book comes from our desire to find a way into the realm of spiritual values that inspire educational leaders. From countless conversations with principals, from essays they've written, from the rich tapestry of artwork they've created, and from artifacts they've shared, we discovered an alluring trove of stories revealing leaders' divine purposes in the form of three spiritual archetypes or personal myths. Archetypes represent universal, often idealized symbols that describe human experience and assist in the shaping of one's worldview (Kreffing & Frost, 1984).

The *Touchstone* leader represents the unwavering focal point of vision for his or her school community, frequently recognized by colleagues, students, and parents as the steadfast decision maker and change agent dedicated to moving the school culture forward. The *Advocate* is best characterized as the champion for a cause beyond oneself, routinely driven by an unswerving commitment to equity and fairness. The *Advocate* recognizes the school as a microcosm of larger society and is devoted to improving individual lives, communities, and institutions. The *Parent* symbolizes the archetypal leader who is admired as the icon of an ethic of care. This is the leader whose approach to his or her work is influenced by an instinctual desire to build relationships and nurture the educational community, to encourage people to discover their hidden talents in an environment of trust and support.

These archetypes are represented by what Paulo Freire (1986) called "thematic universes," or conceptual beliefs that stimulate leaders' desires and dreams as individuals and as professionals. As personal myths, the archetypes represent core themes that are perpetuated throughout peoples' lives. In another sense, we've discovered their spiritual intelligence, evidenced by unconscious insights about their personal journeys. "As the individual begins to reflect on his life through the archetypes and mythological images common to mankind, his awareness may begin to shift to a more universal perspective" (Wilbur, 1979).

When our leaders reflected on their metaphors, they discovered a new province for learning. Not only were their metaphors products of the imagination, but they also represented a process or avenue in which leaders could access personal myths or generative themes that instructed and guided their moral purposes.

The historical associations our leaders cherish as important lessons are enhanced in memorable tales and images that influence the relationship between their spirituality and school leadership. How connected they felt to issues beyond and within themselves and how well they aligned their public and private lives with deep and compelling values are all part of what Sousa (2003) called spirituality. We agree with his contention that all leaders are driven by the forces of spirituality. Our book discusses how the leaders we met translated their core values by way of metaphor into the following constellation of generative and spiritual themes.

- A cause beyond oneself
- An ethic of care
- A sense of purpose, reliability, and dedication to the school community
- A conviction to inspire others to seek their full potential
- An unconscious and compelling need to fulfill strong and intimate beliefs

We thought a lot about Janet Surrey and her colleagues from the Stone Center who studied female growth and development. They acknowledged a struggle to find a meaningful language to formulate and expand on the ideas and experiences of women. Rather than continue to search for alternative channels to explain women's history, they acquiesced to, in their words, "our old and awkward language." From our dialogues with leaders, however, we were surprised when metaphors revealed a provocative and powerful vehicle for describing both women's and men's deep and often unconscious convictions.

Our exploration and experimentation with imagery involved the integration of individual experiences, attitudes, values, and beliefs. Metaphoric thinking enabled our leaders to bring all those fragmented and compartmentalized elements together into the form of generative themes. Their subsequent reflection on those themes activated profound and enduring truths about their intrinsic purposes.

The unifying theory that merged the constellation of core beliefs and themes that perpetuated leaders' personal and professional behaviors was characterized by personal myths. The creation of personal myths evolved developmentally from identifying central themes of experiences, feelings, images, and behaviors that served as the primary motivation for the ways in which leaders behaved in the past and present. By revealing those myths through metaphoric reframing, these men and women gained a new sense of personal history and professional legacy that was transformative and inspired them with renewed energy and resolve.

In the first three chapters we've provided reflective essays as exemplars by school leaders to reveal the three archetypes: the Touchstone, the Advocate, and the Parent. These chapters address the purpose of the book by providing specific examples of each leadership archetype.

We'll also include in each section a developmental story about David, a principal whose professional journey characterized each of the archetypes and dramatized the progressive process associated with metaphoric reframing. We believe David's metamorphosis can be useful in the workplace to spur discussion "outside the box."

Each of the first three chapters will conclude with a reflection about the leaders we've selected and ways for readers to integrate these stories with their own professional work. We will also anchor these archetypes to the Interstate School Leadership Licensure Consortium (ISLLC) standards developed by the Council of Chief State School Officers (CCSSO), whose goals are as follows:

> to stimulate vigorous thought and dialogue about quality educational leadership among stakeholders in the area of school administration. A second intent is to provide raw material that will help stakeholders across the educational landscape (e.g., state agencies, professional associations, institutions of higher education) enhance the quality of educational leadership throughout the nation's schools. (Council of Chief State School Officers, 1996)

To remain consistent with the intent of this book, we'll also provide a variety of lenses and conceptual constructs for readers to reframe their thinking about leadership behaviors.

Chapter 4 focuses on metaphoric reframing as a vehicle for creative leadership. We look at significant writers who've written compellingly about leadership and discuss how their work instructed and inspired our perspectives and theories. Our analysis of the stories and metaphors created by leaders suggested to us that personal myths were responsible for the ways in which these individuals behaved and acted on their core values. Chapter 4 explains the relationship between metaphors and myths and their contribution to effective and compassionate leadership in schools and organizations.

Chapter 5 identifies practical applications of conceptual thinking through metaphor and organizational strategies for effective change. By the time you've finished reading our book and engaging with the activities, we trust that you'll have gained a clearer sense of who you are as a leader and how to enhance your repertoire with new and creative skills. Ultimately, we hope you'll discover a newfound sense of your own history that will inspire your professional work and enrich your personal life.

The Touchstone

1

Standard Bearer and Institutional Anchor

During our conversations with principals, it became apparent that many viewed themselves as leaders with a clear mission to develop exemplary schools by nurturing adult and student learning. The *Touchstone* archetype represents leaders recognized for their experience, expertise, and reflective nature. As symbols of stability, reliability, and trust, Touchstone leaders acknowledge that learning communities must embrace change in order to excel as contemporary organizational cultures.

A number of leaders with whom we spoke created metaphors that resonated with the Touchstone archetype. The *Quiltmaker* is an elementary school principal who viewed her work initially as the eye in the center of a hurricane with a multitude of school issues spinning off and around her. Yet as she continued to play with metaphor, she realized that the essence of her leadership was best characterized by the notion of putting patches together to create a large quilt that represented the school. Her perspective was to look holistically at the full dimensions of her milieu and to fashion from that fabric a mosaic of attitudes, skills, and commitments she adeptly wove into a common vision and sense of purpose. Subsequent to her interview, the Quiltmaker was energized and felt compelled to create an acrostic poem that enhanced her leadership metaphor while simultaneously connecting the patchwork of behaviors that defined her work:

Simmering like a pot of stew—always thinking

Undulating like a snake—constant motion—stretching the limits—moving sideways and then forward

Zesty like a spicy cinnamon stick—challenging minds

Ably facilitating

Nurturing like a mother—allowing her children to venture with the knowledge that school, like home, is a safe harbor

Contrast the Touchstone archetype with a middle school principal's metaphor as the *Public Piñata*. "While I see myself as an agent for change," he says, "I recognize the responsibility inherent in accepting criticism when moving us forward." His focus is encouraging new ideas, allowing safe risk-taking with curriculum development and grant writing for technology integration. He points proudly to a number of curriculum innovations that have inspired his teachers and students. A Fresh Pond unit created opportunities for teaming that led to additional interdisciplinary planning and instruction. A new literacy collaborative with a local university also informed pedagogy at his school.

While he is keenly aware of his critics from the community, the Public Piñata understands that it's his job to serve as a heat shield, to protect his staff from the distractions of pervasive community disapproval for educational initiatives he views as addressing the needs of both his students and his faculty. Rather than reacting to the pressures of dissatisfaction, this principal recognizes the transient nature of his community's initial distrust of educational innovation. As a Touchstone archetype, the Public Piñata understands that "positive educational change often takes time."

The *Leader of the Lesson of the Geese* characterizes himself as an overachiever who focuses on accomplishment through change, "one kid, one parent, one teacher at a time." His military background instructs his sense of responsibility as a junior high school principal. "I've made staff changes, space changes, and program changes," he acknowledges proudly. "My goal is to develop a climate of achievement and success, to change the image of our school." As the new leader of the school, he is adept at identifying a pervasive attitude among staff that the status quo is OK and doesn't require improvement. "Good enough always has to be better," he states. His vision is to change adult expectations of themselves and their students, and he draws on the theory of the geese to drive his point home.

As a 20-year army pilot, he likens his new work to the formation of a flock of geese. He admits there's a paradox with the image. "While I believe leadership should be shared, it's my job to be the one leading the way. If someone falls out of formation, it's my responsibility to make sure they get support. The formation of the geese means everyone steps up to take the lead because we all know the vision." As a Touchstone archetype, this leader is invested in change that focuses on shifting people's views of themselves and inspiring a more community-based mission and sense of school pride.

The *Climate Design Engineer* is an elementary school principal who acknowledges his strong spiritual belief about the inherent value of people. He points to a list of the school's core values posted on the wall in his office. Under Community it states: "We believe our lives are richer when we are part of a community. That community can be as small as our family or school, as large as our country or world. Our community is strengthened when we cooperate, respect community standards, include everyone, resolve conflict and give of ourselves in a spirit of service."

Spiritual values are at the heart of this leader's intrinsic beliefs. He is a devout Roman Catholic who prepared for the priesthood prior to becoming an educator. "Each human being is a reflection of God's love," he says. "That's how I see every person." This personal credo underscores the school vision. It's what led to the establishment of the school's core values. He confides that his predecessor was controlling and created distrust among the staff. Conflicts arose between groups within the school and frequently characterized the interactions between faculty members. Cliques evolved in response to the former principal's directives.

When the Climate Design Engineer became principal, his primary aim was to unite the staff. "I discussed with teachers what I would do to change the atmosphere in the building and elicited from them what they would also do. From those discussions, people began working more collaboratively." He discussed a variety of accomplishments that demonstrated the new sense of unity and pointed to an evaluation rubric he and the faculty developed as an example of his sense of shared leadership. "By showing people I cared about them personally and professionally, we developed a level of trust that has allowed me to move our school in a more positive direction educationally and institutionally. It's my responsibility to ensure none of us waver from that purpose."

EXEMPLARS OF THE TOUCHSTONE ARCHETYPE

To understand more profoundly the dimensions of the Touchstone archetype, we have provided two essays by principals willing to share their perspectives with our readers. We felt it was important to listen to the voices of those leaders in our schools who model reflective thinking about their work and who have discovered metaphor as an informative language for exposing the spiritual values and personal myths that have influenced their professional journeys and accomplishments.

The *U.S. Ambassador of Change* represents perhaps the most powerful illustration of the Touchstone archetype. This middle school principal continues to be informed in best instructional and administrative practices. She is reflective about her role as an institutional leader. She is admired for her sensitive consideration of student and adult needs. Her leadership style reflects a commitment to provide clear direction, remaining steadfast and devoted to the change process in the face of resistance. During challenging and confusing times, the U.S. Ambassador of Change is undaunted. She exudes confidence that problems can be creatively addressed when viewed as opportunities for learning and growth. Her ability to describe the relevance of her metaphor to her professional work represented for us an inspired piece of writing and an insightful reflection for readers to consider.

We also introduce David, a principal in his eighth year as leader of his school. David's representation as a Touchstone archetype provides a different context for how an individual relies on their unique blend of strategies to move their organization forward. In David's case, he attempts for the first time to use metaphoric reframing to expose an old pattern of negative responses to issues of change confronting his school. David introduces us to a metaphor not uncommon in many of our schools today: the victim mythology.

U.S. AMBASSADOR OF CHANGE

by Kathleen Laureti

Whether situational or physical, controlled or imposed, change is an inevitable ingredient of life. The benchmark of an effective school leader is often measured by her relationship *with* and *to* this evolutionary phenomenon. Indeed, no experienced administrator can negatively answer the question "While serving as a principal, has anything changed?" because the very nature of education is fraught with planned and unplanned, predictable and unpredictable occurrences.

Despite the body of literature that has been written about both leadership and the process of change, I have observed that the manner in which a school official *reacts to, promotes, plans, orchestrates, implements,* and *finesses* change is uniquely individual and embedded within the ethos of her culture. The manner is endemic to her core values about people, their dispositions, and their level of collaboration. And because education is a people enterprise, it is incumbent upon the leader to view change not as a maelstrom for admonishment but as an opportunity for courtship. Hence a metaphor for school leadership: I have become an "ambassador," because the connotation is synonymous with diplomacy.

Personal History

Recent life changes have given shape and substance to this philosophy. Well into the adolescent phase of school leadership, having survived my six years of administrative infancy, I was suddenly faced with a life-threatening brain aneurysm in April 1999. It shook my world and forced me to stop, think, and consider. This life change imposed the issues of rest and soul-searching upon me. Prior to this event, I was far too busy for contemplation and self-reflection. Needing only caffeine and nicotine for energy, my metabolism allowed me to race through each day with the energy of an adolescent and embrace each evening with similar ebullience. My 15-week hiatus from the educational foray, however, created a dance for another day . . . something softer, more graceful and contemplative, perhaps a waltz rather than a jitterbug.

It was also during these weeks of rest and reflection that I was asked by the eighth grade class of 1999 to be their keynote graduation speaker. As this was to be my first venture outside my home since the surgery, my confidence level was extremely low, as was my choice for topics. I was convinced that the nuances of brain surgery were not appropriate for an adolescent celebration. Drawing upon childhood experiences, my relationships with my family, sibling jealousies, and our 13 moves up and down the eastern seaboard causing me to attend three different high schools, I settled on the topic of my Italian father's rise to successful graduation from MIT as a fitting graduation speech.

While involved in the writing, I gave deep thought to my dad, his brilliance, and his determination, preservation, and devotion to education. Overcoming his own lack of confidence and poverty, he braved his frontiers and advanced in degrees, finally earning a PhD from MIT. Surely I too could overcome my lack of confidence and give the class of 1999 a speech robust with meaning and substance. I delivered a message to those students, parents, and faculty members for which many stood to applaud and some even shed a tear or two. After my speech I was sent immediately back to the couch for another five weeks of recuperation.

As I rested I continued to think of my father, who apparently had given me gifts I never even realized: quiet determination and a commitment to inspire people by recognizing their strengths rather than their weaknesses. During these weeks of contemplation the fog dissipated, and I became more focused, more visionary, and more in rhythm in both the personal and professional realms, for the connection between the two is virtually symbiotic.

They say that things happen in threes, and my life in 1999 exemplified this adage, for I first developed the illness, I later experienced an epiphany, and by midsummer I was offered a new principal position and a chance to dance, if you will, the dance of diplomacy. No time was more perfect. Still smarting from their brief but highly charged previous administration, the staff at my new school had abandoned ship in large numbers. One-third of the teachers had resigned, some for parallel positions elsewhere, others disillusioned and discouraged with the profession. Several remaining staff members were angry and felt betrayed that their new leader had stayed only one year, having concluded that there was a pathology among the teachers that was contagious and counterproductive to all reform efforts.

In a school functioning for 25 years under the same principal, the teachers, then finding themselves embroiled in the midst of imposed and radical reform for one year, were quite skeptical, and rightly so, of yet another new principal. Before unpacking my boxes, I drafted an introductory memo to vacationing staff members telling them of my appointment, my summer schedule, and my interest in meeting with them to talk "school." Many accepted my offer.

There seemed to be no end to their subjects of conversation, and most of their questions asked the same thing: "What is your leadership style, and how will you treat people?" Their message was crystal clear to me: would I choose to *pump them up* or *tear them down*? From the outset, I selected the former and listened to them with interest. I maintained a journal and actively recorded each conversation. Working from a template that I had designed, I documented the major points of each conversation and used this information to formulate my opening statements at the first faculty meeting on August 30, 1999.

Realizing that we *all* had been wounded either figuratively or literally, I focused my message on the needs of the middle school student. I was optimistic in relating our collective approach to students, yet cognizant of my need to be supportive and compassionate with staff while understanding the "magic" they perform each and every day. Weaving the words of Maya Angelou in her opening comments to the nation's educators at the 1993 ASCD Conference in Washington, D.C., into my speech, I told my staff that "working with middle school children is doing God's work, and each of you should be instantaneously canonized when your time comes."

With her inspiring words still ringing in their ears, my reluctant staff quite nervously began to express their passion, their experience, and their wisdom. It was a good way to begin a new year, and I felt excited to be able to relieve their anxiety and direct them toward a positive future. My exuberance was not unlike the feeling I had experienced just two months earlier while addressing the middle school graduates and expounding on the virtues of my father's determination, bravery, knowledge, and definition of self . . . or at least an idea of what my self could become.

Five years hence I reflect upon my metaphor and why I liken myself to an ambassador. I think about the consistency I have brought to my school, the empowerment and latitude I have given teachers, the respect I have for their individual genius and collective brilliance. I think of the many changes we have lived through . . . those we have embraced and others we have endured. I believe we are all stronger for having survived them.

Working Metaphor

It is fairly easy and very beneficial to extend goodwill and dance the "diplomatic waltz" when one's staff members are feeling good about the work that they do and when public perception is positive and supportive. It becomes increasingly more challenging to offer ambassadorial feedback when people, programs, and policies are under attack. In the fall of 1999, public perception of our middle school was fairly positive. The previous administrator had put into practice many new policies and procedures for the betterment of students, and although internally staff members were still recovering from the myriad of changes, externally we were viewed as progressive, visionary, and far more student centered.

Given this upward trend in public perception, I thought I would continue to foster this forward thinking by embarking on a curricular mapping quest. As the new principal, I was curious to see our curriculum and the manner in which educators approached curricular issues. Utilizing the research of Heidi Hayes Jacobs, I ordered her book for everyone, presented workshops, and trained teachers. I provided opportunities for faculty to converse about *what* they teach and *when* they teach.

After much discussion and rich dialogue, I asked staff to analyze their results and draw some conclusions, hoping our conclusions would be similar. They realized there were areas within the curriculum that were duplicated and other sections of the curriculum where extreme gaps existed. As a united faculty we set out to right these wrongs, by eliminating all duplication and filling in the gaps; we also created assessment instruments that asked students to rehearse, apply, and extend their knowledge. We formed essential questions for each subject area and coordinated our work with the state frameworks. With most people sharing the vision and the purpose, we continued until we felt that many of our core curriculum areas were solidified and were ready to be integrated.

Teachers felt good about the work they had done. They were invigorated and excited to begin making the necessary changes for a spiraling curriculum that built on students' previous knowledge and skills. As I reflect on the success of this endeavor, I am cognizant of the timing, structure, purpose, and balance of the initiative. Timing was important because people were ready to continue their upward trend under a new leader with a new agenda. Likewise, they welcomed a structure that valued research, provided resources and training, and created opportunities for experienced educators to dialogue with one another. Results were immediate, and remedies were quickly sought.

Through the ensuing years, I have had many opportunities to deal with the concept of change and to dance the dance of diplomacy. In those instances where I *controlled* the phenomenon of change, I could set the stage, choose the moment, prepare the staff, and orchestrate the initiative with minimum difficulty. I could delegate tasks and capitalize on the strengths of each participant. I could rely on previous successes and reflect on those journal entries to provide guidance and direction. Hence I could be the ambassador and extend a glad hand to those responsible for implementing change.

Stressed Metaphor

Unfortunately, there have also been many instances in which the metaphor has failed drastically, and the thoughts behind it, despite their good intentions, have faded into nothingness. Taking center stage are all the changes that have been imposed in an untimely and ambiguous fashion, those mandated by the state or federal agencies that have legal implications and tentacles that seem to multiply over time. I refer specifically to those unexpected and situational changes that leaders must massage and finesse as they create a path of least resistance.

The stress involved in this metaphor is often coupled with the realization that one cannot be a goodwill ambassador in every situation, for education is not a hard science, and despite the wealth of seminal research that abounds on every subject, most positions can be argued. Given the multitude of issues facing educational leaders in this new millennium—high-stakes testing, equal access to the curriculum, assessment, and community perception—seldom are we afforded the luxury to plan, strategize, market, and finesse each change that comes our way.

One particular example of a time when goodwill failed to motivate, inspire, or even encourage teachers was when I shared with my lead teachers the idea of reinstating a long-forgotten administrative policy. This policy asked students to evaluate their teachers twice a year using a well-crafted rubric. As a principal who advocates private and personal reflection, I did not require that the results be shared with me. Rather, I wanted teachers to listen to their students and value their input as a means of further improving their teaching practice. Student voices are powerful, and many educational leaders believe students, families, and the community serve as our customers; therefore they should be given an opportunity to state their opinions. As my present school exemplifies a community school, I expected that staff—in particular my lead or "master" teachers—would share my belief.

However, it was soon clear that my teachers were clearly not sharing my point of view and that my powers of persuasion and articulation were not working. After heavy dialogue followed by a heated debate, I mandated that all teachers have their student evaluations of themselves completed before checking out at the end of the year. I further stated that, in the future, *all* staff would have their first student–teacher evaluations completed before the end of the first semester. Likewise, in an effort to model behavior, create equity, and restore balance, I mentioned that I too would value their feedback of my performance as their principal.

As I wrote these pages, reluctant staff members were beginning to conduct these evaluations. I had to resign myself to the fact that not all decisions are popular ones . . . similar to the manner in which L. Paul Bremer, the overseer of Iraq's reconstruction, must have been anticipating his post in Iraq. For although a skilled negotiator, his *goodwill* was not without limits, as he faced the challenge of creating the trappings of a democracy while ensuring that a fundamentalist Islamic government did not win control over the country. I was pondering just exactly what Mr. Bremer might have been willing to risk for the sake of modeling behavior, creating equity, and restoring balance, for as I believe the U.S. Ambassador is a doable and even valiant metaphor, over time any image becomes tarnished, and it is clear that leaders—all leaders—must revisit their relationship *with* and *to* this phenomenon of change to restore clarity of vision.

REFLECTIONS ON THE U.S. AMBASSADOR OF CHANGE

When words do not come easily to the page, some often start by examining words and word relationships. If you head to www.dictionary.com and type in *ambassador,* you'll see the familiar definitions. However, when you examine the word through a thesaurus, some interesting relationships are revealed. Under the entry *agent, ambassador* is listed as a synonym, and the only antonym provided is *principal.*

As our Ambassador is a diplomat or the highest-ranking official, it's interesting to note how she operates. Even in her style of writing, the Ambassador gathers and states the facts: "change is an inevitable ingredient of life." The Ambassador assesses the conditions of the environment and responds accordingly.

The Ambassador also chooses powerful words that have meaning and carry strength, words that cannot easily be misinterpreted. As she reflects on her gifts, she identifies the qualities of "quiet determination," "recognizing strengths," "visionary," and "focus." The Ambassador communicates from inner strength and conviction. There is never panic or put-downs. Even through a whirlwind of events and emotions, the Ambassador understands the endgame and navigates toward that end.

The Ambassador also inspires and listens. Through the use of words and the ability to trust and assess through observation, the Ambassador keeps a pulse on the issues, taps into common goals, and calls upon people's talents to achieve a desired outcome. The Ambassador uses a template, documents major points, and formulates a game plan to execute a diplomatic process for change.

The Ambassador realizes that curriculum alignment is needed in her school. Operationally, she brings a firm process to the situation: collect data, understand the lay of the land, educate, work, and change. This is the Ambassador at her finest, engaging participants to understand a process and work toward a goal.

However, being an Ambassador is not always easy. If anything, the Ambassador must have great nerve and fortitude. Many times she must negotiate diplomatically through waves of emotions and fears. But there is no moving the Ambassador from the fundamental objective, in this case, improving the quality of school. The Ambassador imposes a heavy hand. How will the staff respond? Change might not be what her staff wants right now, but we get a glimpse that, in the end, it will lead to improvement for all.

No doubt the reflections by the U.S. Ambassador of Change characterize a leader with vision for whom the complexities inherent in school leadership are daunting. Her quest to provide consistency and forward thinking within the prevailing context of change manifests her awareness of the challenges confronting all schools today. She is wise and simultaneously humble in accepting her mission to find the rhythm that creates personal and professional harmony. While her metaphor is synonymous with diplomacy, it's clearly of the passionate kind.

This Ambassador exemplifies the focal point that moves her organization with, as well as in spite of, faculty acceptance and support. As a Touchstone leader, she relies on a repertoire of skills and dispositions "cognizant of the timing, structure, purpose, and balance of the initiative."

The Ambassador sustains a commitment to control the dynamics of change by adeptly orchestrating appropriate introductions and preparations necessary to encourage her teachers' continued development individually and as part of a school culture. She qualifies as a Touchstone because she assumes a certain humility as a fallible leader. She's reflective and aware of her shortcomings. She's mindful and appreciative of her journey from administrative infancy to adolescence. And now she's approaching another milestone and reflective phase: administrative midlife.

Thinking back on her trials as an emergent leader, the Ambassador acknowledges mistakes and limitations, but she's not paralyzed by them. To the contrary, failure to the Ambassador and to a Touchstone leader represents a form of empowerment. It is permission to forge ahead to continued development for herself and her faculty, to find applications of personal and communal learning in undoubtedly new and unforeseen contexts.

Goertz (2000) conducted a study to determine the relationship between effective leaders and creativity. She used eight variables based on an extensive review of research studies to characterize effective leaders who think creatively. It's interesting to note the Ambassador's behaviors in light of Goertz's leadership characteristics:

- Passion for work: The Ambassador demonstrated an unwavering conviction to championing the mission of her school. She was passionate in her commitment to children and adults and to creating a full community of learners. Her reference to the inspiring words of Maya Angelou in her opening comments to her faculty opened the doors to their expression of their own passion for teaching and an appreciation for their individual experiences and collective wisdom.

- Independence: While the Ambassador displayed independence of thinking, she was mindful of the impact her decisions had on her faculty. While she valued shared decision making in some instances, it was clear that the Ambassador reserved the right to forge a vision for the school and to move people in that direction in the face of opposition, anxiety, and resistance.

- Goal setting: The Ambassador was clear about her objectives and pursued them with vigor. She understood the complexities of school change but was not deterred from her mission. Throughout the unfolding of each event surrounding her desire for change, the Ambassador remained focused on her goals and continued to reflect them back to her staff. Note also how the power of her own metaphor is used by the Ambassador as a permanent anchor to her personal and professional mission: "I believe the U.S. Ambassador is a doable and even valiant metaphor . . . and it is clear that leaders—all leaders—must revisit their relationship *with* and *to* this phenomenon of change to restore clarity of vision."

- Originality: The Ambassador is devoted to considering ways for teachers to understand their level of effectiveness. She takes a risk by acknowledging that students' voices are powerful and should be heard. Therefore she mandates student evaluations of teachers against a wave of reluctance. Yet she's willing to walk the talk, and in an effort to honor equity and restore virtue, she encourages faculty feedback of her performance as well.

- Flexibility: Notice how the Ambassador deftly negotiated the faculty's assessment of their curriculum to identify problem areas long ignored. Notice how, through that looking together process, the faculty united around a commitment to create assessment instruments that asked students to "rehearse, apply, and extend knowledge." The process of developing and solidifying a core curriculum was enhanced when teachers shared a common vision and purpose. It was a dramatic example of a leader encouraging her staff to generate a variety of ideas to address curriculum challenges that implied everyone's need to adapt to change.

- Wide range of interests: The Ambassador thrived on rich dialogue and reflection with her staff. She understood the importance of accessing the perspectives and wisdom of her colleagues to develop solutions. Her phrases "individual genius" and "collective brilliance" characterized her perception of the faculty and her appreciation for the contribution they all made to improving the quality of their school.

- Intelligence: The Ambassador prided her leadership on intellectual curiosity by posing questions, taking risks, and developing a school community that valued dialogue. Her metaphor reveals serious thought about her journey as an individual and as a professional. She is conscious of her faults and failures and appreciates their purpose to provide lessons about the ways she leads. As an experienced educator and dedicated learner, the Ambassador models reflective practice and sense of purpose.

- Motivation: Is there any question that the Ambassador is a highly engaged and motivated individual? She exudes self-confidence to others while sometimes harboring self-doubt. She is enthusiastic and encourages her teachers to move beyond their comfort levels to seek improvement. The Ambassador is achievement oriented and determined to conceptualize and actualize ways to bring about change.

INTRODUCING DAVID

Phosphorescence! Now there's a word to lift your hat to! To find the phosphorescence, that light within, that's the genius behind poetry.

—Emily Dickenson

In his book *Squirrel, Inc.* (2004), Stephen Denning discusses the importance of storytelling by organizational leaders for coping with change and getting results in an increasingly complex world. Denning claims that "the ability to tell the right story at the right time can have a pivotal impact on the success or failure of any major change effort" (p. xviii). He discusses six positive results stories create in organizations: (1) they spark action, (2) they communicate who you are as a leader, (3) they get people working together, (4) they tame the grapevine, (5) they demonstrate the leader's knowledge, and (6) they lead into the future through rejuvenation and innovation.

To introduce David to readers, we begin with his decision to tell his personal story of tragedy to his faculty. As a leader, David has an intuitive sense that to move his veteran staff from complacency requires dramatic action on his part. He knows he wants to encourage risk taking and openness to change and realizes it's his job to model the desired behavior.

The faculty knew David lost his sight in one eye when he first became an administrator at the school. But they weren't aware of the root causes, the history of reflection David went through, and his discovery of former self-limiting beliefs that resulted from years of introspection.

The following story is what David shared with his faculty. It represented on one level a leader's attempt to create a spark for organizational and cultural change within the school. On another level, David's story symbolized a personal rite of passage by recognizing the significance of his healing and the subsequent acting on his newfound sense of self.

David's Story

In German my last name means looking glass or mirror. It's an apt metaphor for the ways in which I've tended to reflect on my life experiences and direction. My educational inclinations were influenced by personal experiences with Jean Piaget, Martin Luther King Jr., and Dr. Benjamin Spock. Although they helped shape the contours of my professional and personal development, the road I've taken to becoming a school leader has often been arduous and complex.

Gazing through the mirror of my life, I realize my professional and spiritual journeys were launched on an entwined and circuitous path 35 years ago. I was living in Hell's Kitchen, New York City, teaching at an elementary school in central Harlem. One morning as I was waiting on the subway platform, I noticed that the sight in my right eye was beginning to fade. Probably some minor irritation or infection, I thought. Within six weeks, however, the vision was gone. The doctors said it was retina bulbous neuritis, an inflammation of the optic nerve. They didn't tell me the condition was a precursor to something worse.

I continued to teach in New York until four years later, when I moved out of the city and purchased my "restoration project," a two-hundred-year-old farmhouse in Vermont. It was a good metaphor for me—my life was in reconstruction mode. Living in the country awakened a new connection to nature and a simpler way of living.

Life was good, I thought. I liked teaching in the country and felt like I belonged for the first time to a community. I was married and eagerly awaiting a call from the state adoption agency announcing the arrival of our infant son. Unfortunately, my euphoria was short-lived.

It was one of those raw, dreary days that chill to the bone during gray November. Hating to leave the comfort of my flannel sheets, I forced myself out of bed that morning and touched the side of the wood stove in our bedroom. I could see the waves of heat rolling off the stovetop, but for some strange reason I could barely feel the hot metal with my right hand. I noticed the worn floorboards felt cold and abrasive to my left foot, but the other foot couldn't feel a thing.

When my condition didn't change, I went to the local hospital a few days later. The physicians were as confused as I. During the next six weeks, they were unable to explain what was happening as I slowly began to lose control of the right side of my body.

Back in 1975, there were no MRIs to diagnose my condition, but when I mentioned my previous experience with lost eyesight, a lightbulb went on for my neurologists. They concluded the optic nerve incident was a precursor to having multiple sclerosis. They couldn't predict whether the disease would worsen or stabilize. Only time would tell, they said.

I sought therapy to address my anger, shame, and confusion. Therapy provided another lens or mirror for looking within. Gradually, I became acquainted with a darker and more compelling side of myself. It was characterized by the acceptance and integration of what my therapist called the victim mythology. Victims, she said, rarely take responsibility for the frequent pattern of crises in which they find themselves. Instead, they tend to blame others or fate, much like my reaction to MS and to my years of conflict with others in the workplace and sometimes at home.

During this period of gradual awakening, I became principal of a school in western New Hampshire. My health had improved. I no longer limped. I had full motion and dexterity with my right hand. The lost eyesight was the only physical remnant of past afflictions. But my epiphany didn't occur until a casual conversation with a colleague on the playground one day at school.

"I just don't get it, David," she said. "You're such a visionary as a school leader. Don't you find it strange the MS affected your sight?"

Her observation stunned me. This was a connection I hadn't made before. Later, when I reflected on her comment, I realized this was a provocative perspective that shed new light on my physical condition. When I reframed MS as an instructional metaphor, it evolved to a notion of "dis-ease" or discomfort with patterns in my life I was addressing in therapy. The metaphor "dis-ease" freed me from my previous mind-set as victim. I learned that on some level, I was accountable for the development of my "dis-ease" and therefore responsible not only for my healing but for avoiding future episodes of victimization in my life as well.

With the unexpected physical recovery I was making, I began to consider how metaphors can alter a person's as well as an institution's life view, direction, and health. In hindsight, it comes as no surprise that I eventually authored a dissertation exploring personal mythologies of women who principal schools.

That inquiry investigated core and often unconscious themes in three women's lives that influenced their professional purposes and behaviors.

Their personal myths emerged from discussions about their favorite fairy tale characters. Interestingly, the principals in the study were able to recast their fairy tale protagonists as metaphoric representations of themselves: the Badger, the Gypsy, and Everybody's Mother.

I realized that the investigation into the unconscious forces that motivate and inspire school leaders represents no less a shift of mind than what is at the heart of a learning community, namely, a turn from viewing problems as consequences created by someone else or some other forces to accepting how our own actions often contribute to the problems we encounter.

My doctoral studies represented a way to bridge my personal experiences with MS to my work as a school leader. I learned that, throughout history, myths represent metaphors for imaginative explanations of social conditions and human behaviors. Metaphors have a way of reconciling the empirical with the intuitive.

When I completed my doctoral studies and returned from my sabbatical, I began to consider ways for our faculty to look through another lens to address our school system's negative myths. At the time, we were bogged down in district conflicts over contract negotiations, unpopular school board mandates, and complicated curriculum restructuring. I felt that without learning new strategies—changing attitudes, values, and behaviors—our faculty wouldn't be able to take the adaptive steps necessary to thrive in the prevailing environment. On some level, I felt that the sustainability of change depended on having people at our school internalize the change process itself.

We needed a new and resilient scheme for reframing our work context as educators in a system of continual and sometimes destructive change. The more I reflected on my personal experiences and doctoral research, the more convinced I was that metaphoric reframing could be used as a valuable tool for analyzing and producing unique insights about generally complex and often paradoxical trends within our school culture. So eight years after becoming principal, I decided it was showtime for metaphors!

DAVID'S EVOLUTION AS A LEADER, PART 1: CONFRONTING THE VICTIM MYTHOLOGY

The next phase of David's story saw him embark on a new professional journey. He was excited to get back to his school after a yearlong sabbatical. His doctoral thesis had examined the many ways myths influence organizational behavior, and as if by some stroke of coincidence, upon his return, David was confronted immediately with one of the most prominent institutional dysfunctions he had studied and experienced as a veteran administrator, the *victim mythology*.

Prior to the start of the school year, a new contract was negotiated with the teachers' union. A provision in the contract guaranteed all teachers one daily planning period. There was just one problem. While agreeing to the planning time, the school board budgeted for four special coverage teachers when five would now be needed. Up to then, students at David's school participated in physical education twice a week, music and art once a week. These "special" classes allowed teachers time for preparation.

When David convened his first faculty meeting in August, teachers were angered by the school board's failure to fund for the additional coverage. They demanded an immediate resolution. If there was not one forthcoming, they threatened to file a grievance.

During the meeting, David assured the teachers that he supported their need for a daily planning period. When he asked for suggestions to address the issue to avoid a conflict with the board, the only proposal offered was to hire a roving aide to cover the fifth period for each teacher. David acknowledged that this would certainly resolve the contractual issue, but two concerns reflected his rejection of the idea.

David was an instructional leader who always tried to base the impact of organizational decisions on improved student learning. He reflected on the roving aide proposal and doubted that this would ensure a continuation of learning for students. "Having an aide in the classroom to supervise a study hall once a week doesn't provide for the continuous engagement with curriculum for all students. All it does is create an interruption to the steady flow of learning we've come to pride ourselves on."

But David didn't stop there. It was time to put into action what he had spent years investigating and writing about in his dissertation. David reflected on the faculty's customary response to similar issues. Typical of the way labor problems were addressed in their school district, teachers and the school board would get mired in conflict, assume adversarial positions, and ultimately arrive at settlements that usually satisfied only one of the parties. David characterized this behavioral pattern as the victim mythology. "You see," he explained, "the victim is always someone or some group who feels they've been wronged in a grievous way."

David provided examples that described the district's prevailing victimization. There was the adoption of a new curriculum by the board a few years before over the objections of teachers who claimed that there was no connection with the state's mandated frameworks. Rather than provide alternative perspectives for the board to consider, the teachers insisted the curriculum was unrealistic in scope and continued to complain about the issue for years.

Then there was the time the district mandated technology integration in all subjects. Rather than propose strategies and training to instruct teachers about effective practices using technology, teachers argued that they had no time in their school day to meet the new requirement.

"In each of these cases," David concluded, "teachers as well as administrators cried foul but failed to respond proactively with alternative and meaningful proposals that aligned with best instructional practices. We swallowed the bitter pill the board offered and made no attempt to accept any ownership with the outcome of those decisions." What they were left with both times, David reminded them, were failed opportunities to educate the board through dialogue and mutually designed proposals that ensured common purpose and direction.

David called upon the faculty to reframe their thinking about institutional problems. He suggested a new mythology for their consideration. "Think of the heroine or hero in many of the myths and historical events our students study," he said. "Those individuals, whether real or imagined, overcame obstacles by accepting humility and finding positive ways to resolve their problems. They appealed to strong beliefs about fairness, social justice, equality, and ethical values. I propose that we follow their model of heroism for this and future institutional challenges."

While many of the teachers in the room were willing to consider David's suggestion, a core of saboteurs, as David liked to call them, snickered and rolled their eyes in derision. David knew this was a key moment in getting the faculty to move from an old behavioral pattern to trying something new to solve an important problem. So he asked the teachers if there was a time that they remembered when the faculty acted like heroines or heroes to address a problematic issue at school.

After a brief silence and holding his breath for what David felt was an eternity, one teacher recalled the chronic deterioration of the teachers' room years ago. "I remember you asked us to consider ways we could improve staff morale, and we decided to take on the horrible condition of our faculty room." Suddenly teachers smiled and began recounting an assortment of horror stories about the poor conditions that had characterized the faculty lounge. The floor had been disfigured with broken tiles; the bare walls needed spackle and paint; the sink area was always left with lunch trays caked with leftover food; the refrigerator collected remnants of snacks, drinks, and half-eaten meals that looked more like science experiments; and the furniture was old and in disrepair.

"We were mostly concerned that people on our staff took no interest in keeping the faculty room clean," remarked another teacher. "All we would do was either sit around and complain about the slovenly and depressing conditions of that room or just avoid going there."

Even one the "saboteurs" remembered how the staff had created a committee to develop a plan for a refurbished faculty lounge that would provide comfort for staff members, furnish professional articles and journals, display artwork by staff, as well as post a sign-up sheet for members to accept a role in maintaining the upkeep of the room. "It was great," she admitted. "We got all fired up. David found funds in the budget to carpet the room and hire someone to build new cabinets. The district electrician and plumber installed new sinks, a lavatory, and lighting."

David smiled and began to breathe easier. "I'll never forget our celebration breakfast when the room was finally finished," he said. "The room sparkled and so did everyone's eyes when we walked into the lounge that morning. It was a terrific morale booster, a wonderful example of how we took responsibility for a problem and accomplished something absolutely outstanding.

"The thing about victims," David concluded, "is that they tend to be blamers and narrow thinkers. Rarely do they accept ownership for their predicament, and as a result they fail to create meaningful solutions that are positive and conflict free. That's why our faculty lounge existed for so long in such a terrible state."

"Actually," one teacher reflected, "our faculty room was a good metaphor for how we were feeling as a staff at the time. Contract negotiations were stalled, an entire family had committed suicide and devastated all of us, and then there was that group of angry parents who were complaining about school discipline."

David suggested that by adopting the mind-set of a heroine or hero, the faculty would be able to overcome obstacles in a more humane fashion while ensuring the integrity of their school's instructional goals and mission. Furthermore, they would create a model for their school district by implementing a healthier process for problem solving and decision making.

When they began discussing proposals to resolve the planning time issue, David acknowledged that the faculty could file their grievance and surely win. "But what guarantee do you have that the decision in your favor would enhance and improve student learning?" he asked. "I believe we can settle this dispute, embellish our curriculum, and provide a new context for integrating conceptual understandings from the main subject areas. And in so doing," he added, "we would also establish a standard for resolving educational as well as labor issues in our district."

David asked teachers if they would be willing to try this new approach. While some of the chronic resisters remained silent, most of the teachers who had worked with David since the beginning of his tenure trusted his passionate commitment to instructional best practices and his sensitive treatment of children as well as staff. After reaching consensus on his proposal, David divided the faculty into four groups and sent them to different locations for an hour to develop a solution to the planning period issue.

When they reconvened, two groups proposed a dramatic arts instructor while the other two groups suggested a foreign language teacher as the special coverage educator. David congratulated his teachers on their efforts, and after subsequent discussions with the superintendent and the faculty, he and the teachers decided to propose the drama position.

At the faculty meeting prior to the school board presentation, one of the teachers asked David what would happen if the board rejected the proposal. David smiled. "That's easy," he said. "On one level, it doesn't matter, simply because you acted professionally by standing up for the ideals that resonate with our vision of what's in the best interests of students. Worst case scenario is that you file your grievance and most probably win. But what's most important is that we agreed to a new standard for how to address future problems within our school community. No board can take that away. We will have acted as true heroines and heroes."

That evening David and members of the faculty presented their proposal to the school board. David spoke about their effort to find a more meaningful way to address institutional issues without resorting to confrontation that often resulted in dissatisfaction and negative feelings. He complimented the faculty and hoped the board would acknowledge their efforts and welcome the spirit of their professional response.

After some discussion, the school board applauded the teachers and David. They voted unanimously to accept the proposal for a dramatic arts teacher. Everyone was pleased with the positive settlement of this issue. At school the next morning, David and the school spirit committee hosted a celebration breakfast to commemorate the new path they had chosen for teachers, students, and the school.

REFLECTIONS ON DAVID AND THE VICTIM MYTHOLOGY

Name It

There are many different ways to look at David's actions as principal and as a Touchstone archetype. For instance, one of the first strategies David used was to *name the endgame.* David had seen all of this before. A contractual issue, union gets involved and files a grievance, board takes action. The grievance is resolved by definition, and some change is imposed. The solution often disrupts the school more than it helps; the board can say the issue is resolved, it costs some money to resolve the issue, and the end result is that no one is happy or satisfied with the resolution.

Stage 1 of Reframing: Reflecting on the Old Storms

David's strength lies in getting the attention of his faculty. He does this by first *naming the negative process.* Then, he offers another view. In this case, by tapping into his doctoral work. David suggests reframing the issue through the eyes of the hero or heroine. Here was a perfect example of a leader offering a new process and demonstrating some passion about it. The faculty was willing to give it a try, albeit skeptically.

We also catch a glimpse of David's guiding principle: David was an instructional leader who always tried to base the impact of organizational decisions on improved student learning. As a Touchstone principal, he saw the bigger picture. (Our experience also tells us that David must have "walked the talk" many times before for the faculty to "buy into" the notion of a staff of heroes and heroines!)

David uses data. Look at the past issues, he says. What can we learn? What does your experience as a faculty member tell you about our shared experiences with similar problems? Do you really believe following the same process over and over will get you new results? He knows the history of the school and uses it deftly to navigate the faculty toward new but unforeseen horizons.

David knew the existing practice wasn't grounded in the improvement of student learning; rather this was about power and politics between school board and teachers' union. As a Touchstone principal, David was well aware that "power and politics" was a very difficult venue in which to create significant change.

Stage 2 of Reframing: Informing a New History

David then calls on a past experience, a successful endeavor in which the staff had been active participants. The event: refurbishing the faculty room. From the faculty's perspective, this issue was something they cared about. They wanted change and could see a direct benefit for their efforts. But how does this impact student learning? How is David acting as an instructional leader here? This issue proved to be the fundamental cornerstone of David's leadership as a Touchstone principal. He was able to establish trust.

On the surface, redesigning a faculty room may not seem like an important event. But from a learning perspective, this event had all the elements of a successful classroom experience: There was motivation (desire to have a quality place to eat, talk, interact with peers); there was a process (the faculty formed the teams, committees, and workgroups to reach their objectives); and there was a measurable outcome (the redesigned faculty room and the use by staff). What came of this? A celebration organized by many to commemorate an end result that benefited all.

Success breeds success. As David developed trust, he also allowed his staff to build a shared vision around an issue that was important to them, their workplace. Staff morale would be crucial to creating a successful learning environment to improve student learning. By recalling this experience, David is further reminding the faculty that there is a successful process that can be utilized to get desired results. This would become a mantra the faculty would hear again: We've done it before; we can do it again!

DISCOVERING YOUR TOUCHSTONE

Conceptually, a Touchstone leader is both a rock and a rocker. As a rock, he or she is firm and solid in his or her beliefs and vision as a leader. As a rocker, he or she knows how to shake, move, and sway others steadily. Touchstones are reference points for their organizations. Touchstones set the measure for the quality of work that is expected from all members of the institution. They manage change in a positive way by focusing their energies on outcomes while skillfully dealing with elements that distract or confuse.

In practice, Touchstone leaders are committed to novel approaches to instructional and organizational change. They possess the skills and strategies necessary for shaping a sustained focus on their institution's vision. Touchstone leaders model reflective practice by continuing to be informed about best practices in administration and teaching. They are highly regarded by their colleagues and the local community as deft and proactive problem solvers. Exhibiting steadfast devotion to student, teacher, and organizational growth, Touchstone leaders are respected as passionate and forthright anchors for their schools.

Identifying the Touchstone leader in you may seem easy, but this is not about routine or management, it's about leadership. Use the following questions to help identify the Touchstone qualities in you.

1. Name three qualities your staff, community, and students would identify as the values and beliefs characterizing your leadership. Are these management qualities or leadership qualities?

2. How do your Touchstone qualities compare with the vision of your school, district, or organization? Are they aligned?

3. On a scale from 1 to 10, how does your school or organization respond to change? What are the processes and strategies you use to create a culture of change?

4. How do you deal with resistance to change?

5. How are you a "rock" for your institution? How are you a "rocker"?

On the following pages we provided reflection activities that ask questions in different and more provocative ways to elicit deeper understandings about your leadership dispositions. When you've completed them, we invite you to turn back to this page and compare your responses to your answers to the five questions above and to consider how they might have illuminated a new perspective about your work as a leader.

REFLECTION QUESTIONS AND ACTIVITIES

Leadership Self-Assessment

1. Here are the ISLLC (Interstate School Leadership Licensure Consortium) standards for school leaders that are being adopted by most states for certification of school administrators. (See Resource for more comprehensive descriptions.)

ISLLC Standards

I. The Vision of Learning

II. The Culture of Teaching and Learning

III. The Management of Learning

IV. Relationships with the Broader Community to Foster Learning

V. Integrity, Fairness, and Ethics in Learning

VI. The Political, Social, Economic, Legal, and Cultural Context of Learning

Based on the standards, which ones reflect the Ambassador's expertise and weaknesses? How would you compare your ISLLC rating of the Ambassador with yourself?

2. Consider Goertz's eight leadership characteristics that were used to assess the Ambassador's behaviors. Rate yourself based on those variables. What did you learn?

Organizational Development: Reframing

3. Using the **circle map** on the next page (Hyerle, 1996), consider an issue of change you are currently addressing. Name it. Put a frame around it, and in the frame write whatever words come to mind. These words reflect your frame of reference about the issue you are addressing. They are the lenses that influence how you view the issue and what you bring to it based on your experiences and perspectives. Notice who or what is missing from the frame (see the following example on **Assessment)**.

Now create a metaphor for your issue. This is called *reframing*.
Assessment *in our school is like a recipe with some missing ingredients.*

4. In the example you can see the reframing of the issue as a metaphor: "Assessment in our school is like . . . " Reframe your issue. Try this activity with the faculty in small or large groups. Choose the same issue and ask each group to reframe the issue by creating a metaphor after they complete the circle map. What information is gained by looking at the multiple metaphors? Is there a common theme or pattern to the metaphors? How can this information be used to move your organization forward on the issue?

Circle Map—Template

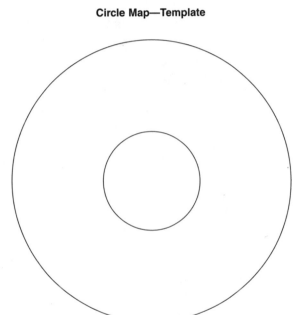

The Advocate

*Proponent of a
Cause Beyond Oneself*

The second leadership archetype, the *Advocate*, represents those school administrators dedicated to a cause beyond themselves. These leaders devote their work to the improvement of humanity and educational institutions. Their sense of purpose is influenced by a set of core values that focus on inspiring students and adults to connect their learning and teaching to worthwhile causes and projects that enhance the local community or contribute to their moral development and social consciousness. These are the leaders who often base their decisions on the best interests of students, teachers, and school staff.

One elementary school principal reflects on her metaphor, the *Cat:* "I'm a loner. I need my space," she says. "Cats are structured that way. They are independent when they want to be. They're warm and affectionate other times."

It seems paradoxical that such a private person is comfortable as a school leader. Yet, the apparent contradiction between her persona and her strong desire to be an advocate for children is not a problem for her. "As a cat, I can sometimes be a lion or a tiger if it means improving the quality of life for kids." She believes leaders have a moral responsibility to work ethically and with integrity. "Sometimes," she says, "I'm not empathetic if what we're doing as educators is not in the best interests of children."

Then there's the *Coach.* "I'm in a place where I can make a difference," she says. She's proud of her veteran staff of elementary school teachers. As a second-year principal, she is finding ways to encourage teachers to consider new instructional approaches that link the formal curriculum with real-life problems in the community and in society. This represents a big challenge, given the school's need to improve its test scores on the state assessment.

"Right now," she says, "we're a team who've been underdogs, but we're not discouraged." She acknowledges her disappointment when the school's appeal to have the state reconsider its test scores in light of improvements to the curriculum was denied. "I told the staff I feel as if I failed them as a leader. But they didn't share that sentiment. They felt I've been here for the students, the teachers, and the community through thick and thin. We hang in there for the kids."

The *Lead Learner* is a principal who has struggled with her self-assessment and the perception of her by others. She admits to projecting self-confidence while remaining sensitive to her vulnerability as a leader. For her, the metaphoric reframing process helped reconcile the apparent contractions she was feeling about her personal and professional personas.

"I see myself journeying along with my staff to improve the quality of this school," she says. By reflecting on herself as a Lead Learner, she's able to recognize how her role has fostered a sense of trust within the school and local community. By acting on her core belief that it's her job to improve the lives of others, she's discovered a comfort level with her leadership vision.

"I've helped people develop new wings," she admits proudly. "My goal to share leadership with the staff has provided opportunities for others to realize skills and talents that were previously unknown to them."

She considers the role of technology in her school as illustrative of how she advances improved learning experiences for both students and adults. "I wanted all students pre-K to eighth grade to have access and ongoing learning experiences integrating technology. I wanted all staff to use technology with greater expertise and comfort. But my expectations were hollow until I was able to model that development and to provide support." She discusses her enlistment of an administrative council of teachers to cultivate professional development, to modify their curriculum, and to create a schedule that subsequently enhanced technology integration. "That," she says with a smile, "is how I've acted as Lead Learner and gained the personal confidence to be an instructional leader."

The *Megaphone* considers her role as a voice for the children, the teachers, and the parents of her school. As a former business manager, school board member, and parent who homeschooled her children, she feels as if she became an educator almost by default. "In each of those roles, I learned early on that people often need a voice, whether it's in the business world, as a community representative, or as an adult trying to help her youngsters make sense of the world. From those experiences, I realized I wanted to speak for those who couldn't speak for themselves."

She reflects on her childhood in an alcoholic family. She talks with emotion about learning to be a survivor. "I realize my values as a school leader are very deep seated." She acknowledges how at times she struggled with the broad spectrum of stakeholders at her school and her need to represent each of them. "Sometimes," she confesses, "my advocacy gets me in trouble. It's important for people to be heard. And if there are some who feel powerless to do so, I'm compelled to speak on their behalf."

The *Utility Player* views her role as primary support person endowed with a repertoire of skills and competencies to assume a variety of roles within the school setting. "I don't ever want to get stale as an educator," she says. "I can go anywhere to work with kids," who, she admits, are sometimes more likable than adults.

The Utility Player is a principal in a large and what she calls an "unwieldy" school district. The nine-member school board is "tough," she says, because of their inconsistent support and their desire to micromanage the schools. "All the more reason," she notes, "to be a relationship builder, to develop their trust and appreciation for what we do for students."

While the work of school administration is often frustrating, the Utility Player is tireless in her efforts to improve the quality of school life for children. "As a caregiver, I am motivated to put new things forward that improve our pedagogy and the learning experiences for our students. I remain current in best practices and am proud of our accomplishments to create programs that link academic learning to team projects that improve our community."

She describes a variety of initiatives that characterize the kind of community-based learning she considers valuable for citizenship development. "I loved the booster club painting our sports field house and locker rooms or the way we included chorus, drama, movement, poetry, art, and technology not as separate parts of the school day but integrated with our content area studies. Those connections between disciplines provide powerful experiences for adolescents as well as skeptical board members who always want to know how our teaching prepares students for the real world."

EXEMPLARS OF THE ADVOCATE ARCHETYPE

"The Evolution of a Metaphor" is a compelling essay characterizing the Advocate archetype. Written by a K–8 principal in a rural setting in New

England, this story traces the historical roots of a leader whose intimate relationship with nature and children reveals the moral tenets of his professional mission and purpose.

The *Gardener* understands his place in the lives of his students and staff. While he acknowledges school as a transient experience, its importance as an institution for improving society is deeply ingrained within his sense of leadership and his commitment to a cause beyond oneself. His students are annuals. They require proper care and expert instruction to prepare for their journey through a lifetime. His teachers are perennials. They ensure stability and progressive refinement of a school culture where classroom learning and real-world applications are entwined. It's the overseeing of this mix of annuals and perennials with fervor that symbolizes how this leader fosters growth and encourages his school to thrive.

We also return to our story about David. In this chapter, we'll observe how he addresses the needs of students with handicaps and the challenge of diversity within the school community. David acts with intention by calling upon his moral principles as an Advocate archetype and his skills as an instructional leader. His journey also dramatizes the way a leader relies on a unique blend of problem-solving strategies to confront critical and complex concerns by linking solutions of seemingly disconnected issues to the school's vision and mission.

THE EVOLUTION OF A LEADERSHIP METAPHOR*

by Richard Jenisch

Throughout my career, I have often called upon the wisdom of those people who, without knowing it, provided me with skill and knowledge that directed both my personal and professional life. I have come in contact with thousands of students, staff, and parents throughout my career, and although my informal study is not scientific, I find that those who

---

*Author's note: I struggled trying to identify a metaphor for my leadership style. That exercise alone caused me to reflect on who I am as a leader and what drives me to do what I do. I have always been aware of the influences on my life and their impact on me as a person but had never considered the connections between those influences and my leadership style.

This process provided me with renewed confidence and validation for my skill as a leader. As a rural school principal, I am somewhat isolated from my peers, and it is easy to lose focus and perspective when confronted with hundreds of decisions and dozens of tasks on the table each day. Developing a metaphor for my leadership style was a process of renewal for me, reminding me to remain strong, to continue to take risks, and to remain committed to comprehensive school reform.

have some connection with the earth possess a wholesomeness, wisdom, intuitiveness, and strength that extend beyond the norm. Their interaction with and their understanding of the earth as a precious commodity gives them a keen sense of how all things in life rely on one another and how fragile each is by itself. I was surrounded by that wisdom growing up. It lies at the heart of my metaphor for leadership.

My grandparents were Austrian immigrants who came to this country in the early 1900s. They were of tough European stock and raised seven children (six boys and one girl) on a small farm in a rural New Hampshire town. After World War II, my father married my mother, a USO volunteer from Massachusetts. We lived on my grandfather's farm for a few years until our nearby house was made habitable, after the nights and week-ends my father worked on it. I grew up with a proud heritage, surrounded by an extremely hardworking family who deeply valued the land and the environment. My early memories of planting and harvesting our two-acre garden, brewing potions to feed the pigs, collecting eggs, mowing the fields, bringing in the wood, canning vegetables, hauling water from the river, smoking meat, and celebrating our work provided me with a con-nection to the earth that has guided almost every aspect of my life.

As a young child, I followed my grandfather everywhere. He was a weaver by trade and worked at the New Hampshire Artistic Web Company. He ran a Jacquard loom and created elaborately designed lace and ribbon. He designed and built many of his own tools and knew the looms inside and out. It was fascinating to visit him at the factory, just down the road on the river, and watch him work. The factory was powered by a waterwheel and by a steam engine with a huge flywheel, which added to my absolute fascination with the place. My grandfather was a master weaver of his trade in the old country, and much of what he made was used to adorn the robes of priests in Europe, including the pope.

In their off-hours, my grandfather and grandmother mowed the fields by hand with a scythe, planted and tended 2 acres of vegetables, man-aged a 20-acre forest, cut 20 cords of wood annually by hand, raised a variety of livestock for food, and canned hundreds of pints and quarts of fruits and vegetables for the winter. I remember whole hams and slabs of bacon hanging in the attic, dozens of bushels of potatoes in the cellar bin, the barrel of hard apple cider that we tasted from time to time, the crocks of sauerkraut, and the varied selection of vegetables and fruits canned almost night and day during the harvest.

I loved to walk the woods with my grandfather. He kept the forest floor as neat as any room in his house. Using a crosscut saw that he kept razor sharp, he cut cords of wood in four-foot lengths that he carted out of the forest on a wheelbarrow. Later in the fall, the family would get together to cut the wood into stove-sized lengths, and my grandfather would split every bit of it with an ax and some wedges, usually working all day long with no substantial breaks. He loved the land and never took for granted what it offered him. His small farm was for him an estate, a plantation offering him something that would never have been possible in the "old country." I can remember him expressing his deep appreciation over and over for the country that provided him the opportunity to own and work the land.

My father worked for Merrimack Farmers Inc., a feed supply business with stores throughout New Hampshire. He worked at a local store and became an invaluable resource to farmers and gardeners throughout the area. I would ride with him as he delivered grain, fertilizer, and other related items to farms across the countryside. I met many hardworking folks who were who they were. They were real. They were hardworking, honest, and trustworthy. I came to understand and appreciate the wisdom that they seemed to draw from the earth. Their soiled and callused hands told a story of strength and commitment, of pride and honor, of principles and values.

I grew up a gardener, just like my father and grandfather. There was something spiritual about planting and harvesting the crop. Nurturing the garden as it sprang to life was exciting, renewing, and strangely comforting. I have never felt at peace as I did when the crops were in and a winter's worth of provisions was safety stored in the house and barn. The soil made me feel connected to something I couldn't really explain but a feeling I sought whenever I felt threatened. It brought both power and humility at the same time.

When I moved away from my roots to attend college, I slowly began to figure out who I was, what kind of person I was, what I wanted in life, and, perhaps most important, what I believed. I began to understand the depth of the lessons I had learned growing up and was able to put them into perspective. I discovered that what I had learned could apply to anything I wanted to do, including teaching, my career of choice.

I have been a teacher, head teacher, assistant principal, and for the last 25 years, a K–8 principal. Of course, I am also a gardener. I plant annuals, perennials, vegetables, trees, and shrubs to balance the landscape at my home and even at my school. In my professional life I seek to create and maintain the same balance. Just as the flowers and vegetables all have unique needs and must be nurtured in a special way to survive and thrive, so do the students. If they do not get what they need, the flowers are not as big and bright as they should be nor the fruit as large and prolific. If their care is overlooked, the garden falls out of balance, and although most find a way to survive, they never really reach their potential. Somehow they survive despite what they experience, but they thrive and reach their potential only when their basic needs are met, and they are nurtured using the right formula for each individual variety. Here lies the metaphor.

It has always been a priority of mine to know as much about my staff and students as possible. I have learned that by observing closely, listening intently, being visible throughout the school day, being available to talk with, and interacting with staff and students in both formal and informal settings, I can learn amazing things about how they think, what they need, and who they are. It allows me to maintain a mental database of information that I can access whenever I have to make decisions or judgments involving any of them. Whether planning professional growth activities, conducting observations, ordering materials, assigning duties, making placements, providing TLC, managing discipline, dealing with crisis, developing schedules, or dealing with virtually any responsibility I have, the task is made easier and more effective because I know and understand my students and my staff as individuals. The perennials and the annuals can only thrive when all conditions are right. A good gardener can spot a problem from a distance because he knows what to look for. As a school principal I can do the same.

I greet students as they get off the bus each morning and welcome my staff as they arrive in the early morning, I can sense if things are in order or out of sorts. It allows me to intervene immediately to provide whatever support is necessary to get that individual through the day. It could mean something simple like dropping off a greeting card of encouragement or providing a hug. It might mean calling a last-minute substitute to cover for a teacher not feeling well or covering a class so the teacher can take care of a personal or professional issue. It might mean sharing words of wisdom or sharing a similar experience and how it was resolved. It might mean offering to sit in on a difficult meeting or mediate a problem the teacher is having with a colleague, a student, or a parent. It might mean taking a few minutes to help a student finish a homework assignment or providing the time, the space, or a resource for completing the assignment before going to class. It might mean reading a story with a child on dealing with bullies, with sadness, with the loss of a pet or a loved one, or with a peer relationship gone wrong. It might mean taking a student home to retrieve glasses, clothing, or lunch. It may mean allowing a student to make a phone call to a parent or grandparent for reassurance or just to make a much-needed connection after a difficult morning. It might mean just applying a bandage or some tender loving care. Whatever the intervention required, simple or involved, it often serves to build strong and trusting relationships that are based on mutual respect and understanding. It cannot take place from behind a desk. Each and every day I walk my property religiously. I check every shrub, every tree, and every plant. I make that same connection at school.

I have always made it a point to look beyond the people I am interacting with in an effort to understand who they are, what contributed to who they are, the source of their motivation to do what they do, and the factors that have brought them to me. I have always found that if I watch and listen long enough, I will eventually find a connection that I can begin to nourish and build upon. With rare exception, this has allowed me to be successful in dealing with any situation I encounter. If you can work through the pretentiousness and the defensiveness to get to the real person, you can begin to build trust and work toward solving problems at all levels.

Although not based on any science, I am convinced that as we drift further away from our environmental roots, a disconnect occurs that once provided people with much more than a bounty to sustain them through the winter. We have experienced a spiritual disconnect that has left us less responsible, less satisfied, and less sure of what is really important in our lives.

I love working my garden at home and my "garden" at school. Both remind me of the miracle of growth and provide me with comfort and a sense of purpose and wonder. When graduation comes each year, I am reminded of the hard work and nurturing it took to get each student to this point in his or her life. As I hand each student a diploma, I am always filled with a sense of deep satisfaction much like the feeling I get when I view my garden in full bloom. It is an emotional time, springtime of course, and the gardens are just beginning to bloom.

REFLECTIONS ON THE GARDENER

All Season Green-Up Tonic
1 can of beer
1 cup of ammonia
½ cup of liquid dish soap
½ cup of liquid lawn food
½ cup of molasses or corn syrup
Mix all the ingredients together in a large bucket, then pour into a 20 gallon hose-end sprayer and apply to your plants.

—Jerry Baker
Great Green Book of Garden Secrets

In the writing of "The Evolution of a Leadership Metaphor" there is an interesting process and need to provide a historic perspective of the generational ties to the land. The history embodies a strong sense of work ethic, pride, respect, and wisdom.

The Gardener as a metaphor for a school leader provokes so many images and thoughts. There are an endless number of plants (annuals and perennials). Vegetable gardens bloom to provide nourishment. Trees and shrubs bring function and form to the landscape, holding soil in place and providing shelter to other plants. The categories within the taxonomy—kingdom, phylum, class, order, family, genus, and species—all help to classify, sort, and help us understand the needs and functions of each plant, all of these botanical wonders taking root in the earth and finding ways to have their needs met in order to flower and bloom. Each mature plant then gives back to the entire system by way of its fruit, seeds, gases, or material. What a dynamic system!

The parallels of the garden to the ecosystem of a school are powerful: trying to figure out what plants we'd like in our garden is like determining what outcomes we want for everyone who attends our school. They're based on the types of soil (physical environment), the weather patterns (climate), and what they are fed (resources).

The tonic at the beginning of this section is integral to this reflection. First, like our administrator, the tonic is made from ingredients that are common and available. The All Season Green-Up Tonic is one that can be applied to everything growing in the yard and garden. Each ingredient alone seems ordinary, but as a mixture these ingredients create a powerful potion. You can see the importance of each ingredient for nourishment, cleaning, prevention, and health. Our administrator also uses his "common ingredients": encouraging words, being available to cover a class, or even a hug. These common ingredients help nourish the faculty and students in his school. But as a gardener he is constantly inspecting every student and staff member, checking the growth, the buds, the flowering mechanisms, and the fruit. He evaluates, assesses, and creates just the right tonic for every individual as required.

We describe this tonic ingredient list to present the resourcefulness of this principal. Many of the ingredients of the tonic can be found in most households; maybe one or two of the items need to be purchased. Our administrator uses this same philosophy to meet the needs of the "seeds" in his school. He strives for student-centered approaches, he makes himself visible and available, and he uses professional development to "fertilize" and promote growth in best practices. He reallocates the limited resources available to him and combines them in unique ways, not just to survive but to "bloom."

The first tonic was a general all-purpose mix that can be used everywhere. But our Gardener knows that often we need a special mixture, because each class of student has different needs. Here is another elixir from the *Great Green Book of Garden Secrets*:

Flower Feeder
1 cup of beer
2 tbsp of fish fertilizer
2 tbsp of liquid dish soap
2 tbsp of ammonia
2 tbsp of hydrogen peroxide
2 tbsp of whiskey
1 tbsp of clear corn syrup
1 tbsp of unflavored gelatin

4 tsp of instant tea
2 gal. of warm water
And for tired old roses add rotten bananas skin and all!

This mix can be for many plants, but the bananas make it just right for the roses (by the way, it's the potassium!). Our principal understands the uniqueness of each of his students. He may not have a degree in chemistry or botany, but his understanding of what is needed and what is right comes from experience and wisdom. He feels a spiritual and genetic connection to his work that is evidenced each year by what was planted in September and what was harvested in June.

The Gardener in this essay is an example of the Advocate archetype. Making use of limited resources in a variety of new ways is the way he advocates the success of all members in his community. He professes not to have "scientific studies" that support his theories, but he is very knowledgeable about the active ingredients: "It might mean offering to sit in on a difficult meeting or mediate a problem. . . ." The active ingredients here are trusting, caring, making the time to be there, and listening. By examining the growth, the Gardener knows through experience what to add and how much to add and takes the necessary action. He assumes responsibility for being the advocate for each and every plant, tree, or shrub in his school.

The Gardener advocate has a spirited work ethic that is not egocentric. The results of his labors can only be measured by the quality of the crops, the fragrance of the flowers, the vibrant colors, and the abundance of the harvest. Most people don't recognize the talents of the Gardener—commitment, expertise, constant monitoring, and attention to detail—but when he is successful we are all very quick to enjoy his work. His reward is his pride in watching others enjoy the results.

DAVID'S EVOLUTION AS A LEADER, PART 2: A WONDERFUL HARMONY IS CREATED WHEN WE JOIN THE SEEMINGLY UNCONNECTED

We now fast-forward David's journey with his teachers to another challenge they experienced five years later. One of the concerns David frequently expressed was addressing the long-standing and seemingly unrelated issues of improving playground discipline, integrating emotionally handicapped and behaviorally challenged students, and enhancing diversity awareness.

The quote in the title of this section about harmony is attributed to Heracleitus. This Greek philosopher believed that everything was "in flux," that change is what is real and stability is more of the illusion. David used reframing as a tool to help his faculty see the relationship between discipline and learning. He helped his staff grow as they began to make connections to issues and processes that initially seemed unrelated to each other. Problems are not often solved by simply replacing elements in the equation. Issues such as discipline are more systemic, and a broader view is often necessary to find a solution.

For years David and the faculty grappled with the issue of discipline in the school. Prior to David's becoming the principal, school conduct was enforced with afterschool detentions, in-school suspensions, and short-term dismissals.

Through a variety of staff-development initiatives and countless surveys on effectiveness, numerous refinements were made to the school behavior plan. Over time, David and his veteran staff gradually began to reframe their notions about discipline. As the faculty became more proficient at designing and implementing a positive behavioral system, students and teachers began to understand that discipline meant to teach and to learn, not to punish. Nevertheless, even with those developments, one area still persisted as a significant challenge: playground recess.

The school took pride in developing the first program in the district aimed at addressing the needs of emotionally handicapped and behaviorally challenged students. While all of the students were successfully integrated throughout the school day, a subtle exclusion of those students was apparent during recesses.

The issue was further complicated by a clause in the teachers' contracts exempting them from playground supervision. Less-trained para-educators were hired at minimum wage to monitor students in groups of 150–200 in an unstructured setting outside. For students with interpersonal and behavioral challenges, the recess program loomed as an unwelcome and often threatening environment. For the paraprofessionals, the playground became the scene of constant settling of disputes, identification of repeat offenders, and frequent reports to teachers about minor skirmishes and infractions.

Everyone was getting upset—parents, students, and teachers. No matter what rules and consequences were created, the problems on the playground continued to proliferate. Teachers began to quarrel about the quality of the supervision and the need for some of them to spend time on the playground. The old victim mythology began to creep into the picture, with some staff members voicing concerns about teachers having to be out on the playground in violation of the contract. Although some of the original saboteurs were no longer at the school, the few that remained pointed their criticism and cynicism at the school board and insisted that the problem could be resolved if the pay scale for recess supervisors was increased to attract more qualified individuals.

David knew that the small group of resisters thrived on conflict, and he was determined to prevent them from influencing the majority of the staff.

He decided it was time once again to ask the faculty to think positively and work with him to find a creative solution that he was sure was within their grasp. For David, it was just a matter of reframing everyone's thinking, including his own. "What if we consider recess to be something different?" he asked. "Suppose we reframed it as an extension of the educational program? What would that look, sound, and feel like?"

Dividing the faculty into groups again, David asked them to convene in different rooms and spend time considering new perspectives about recess time and what it should achieve. As he visited each group, David listened to the discussions and perspectives. Teachers seemed energized and motivated to think creatively about a problem that had persisted and generated tension and conflict within as well as outside the school.

When they reconvened and shared their ideas, the dawning of a new vision about recess began to take form. "We need a name, icon, or metaphor to represent our new concept of what was once recess," David said. "Think about what that might be." Rather than continue with the meeting, David wanted to provide time for teachers to talk among themselves for a week, to let ideas germinate during informal discussions. During that period, David entertained serious reflection and hosted discussions with parents and the superintendent to lay the groundwork of community support for what would eventually be proposed.

Another element of David's personality influenced the outcome of this predicament. He was a firm believer in the concept of synchronicity, or what he called meaningful coincidences. Ultimately, it was a synchronistic event that contributed to the resolution of the recess problem.

After a series of discussions at coffee hours with parents, David received a call from Pat, a mother of two students who attended the school. She requested a meeting to talk about the recess issue. When they met a few days later, David couldn't believe his eyes and ears. Sitting before him was a certified recreation therapist!

Pat was intrigued by the discussion about reframing the concept of recess David had presented at the parent association meeting. While many were skeptical and wanted more specifics, Pat understood what David and the teachers seemed to be considering. After his meeting with Pat, he invited her to a task force selected by the faculty to design a program of activities tied to the curriculum. They proposed restructuring the recess times and suggested new playground equipment to accommodate the events. They also created a plan to improve the integration of behaviorally challenged students as well as children from other countries, who were often shunned by their peers.

At the meeting discussing these new proposals, David was surprised that many of the suggestions offered by teachers paralleled the ideas he, Pat, and the task force had discussed. They decided that the purpose of recess was to enhance the instructional program in an environment that encouraged student participation and cooperation. When the faculty agreed to the general framework of the program, David asked, "So instead of recess, what do we want to call this time of day?" Within five minutes, the staff unanimously agreed: recreation education.

The task force developed a job description for a recreation educator and reviewed it with the faculty. After some refinement by teachers, David took the proposal to the superintendent, who followed the progress of the school's attempt to solve the recess problem. With his support, the proposal was accepted by the school board.

Recently Pat, who was subsequently hired as the recreation educator, was complimented by the city's director of recreation and parks. "In all my years in recreation education, I have never seen, heard, or considered such a concept at a public school," she said. "This is something the town should be proud of. I want to bring Pat to the next national conference of recreation directors and have her discuss her program as a model for other public schools."

Today, recess looks, sounds, and feels very different for the children and adults at David's school. Once a week, Pat brings her golden retriever, Molly, to the playground. Molly attends every recreation education period. Students with behavioral issues are given the responsibility of seeing that Molly gets exercise and plays with other students on the playground. "Molly's a magnet," Pat says. "She draws other kids to her and to the behaviorally challenged students. What a wonderful way to bring children together."

Recently, the science coordinator for the district spent the day with Pat and students on the playground. They learned about energy, motion, and force. On another day, outdoor games from India, Panama, and Russia were taught by the children from those countries.

"Connecting all the pieces" is how David characterized the success of the recreation program to his teachers. "We reframed a problem and created some pretty powerful solutions." He wanted to elicit from the faculty changes they noticed. It was important for the naysayers on the staff to hear from their colleagues how the resolution of this problem was a win-win situation for everyone. "Well," said one teacher, "we definitely enhanced student learning with Shirley [the science coordinator] facilitating those science activities. The kids loved them."

The director of the Behavioral Support Program commented, "My kids are no longer fearful about recess. They look forward to either playing with Molly or being included in some of the games."

One of the paraprofessionals admitted that she felt more confident working with a supervisor. "Pat has skills I don't have. She's a great teacher to me; I feel like I'm part of a team, whereas before I was left to sort things out on my own, and I wasn't very successful or happy."

What was once a source of anxiety for teachers and students at David's school evolved into one of its shining successes. By shifting their image of recess from a traditional construct to a novel context, David and his staff achieved something they couldn't previously imagine. "We're heroines and heroes once again," David reminded everyone. "We accomplished quite a lot with just a twist and a turn of our mind-set." Most on the staff agreed.

REFLECTIONS ON DAVID AND THE PLAYGROUND

Stage 3 of Reframing: Norming a Change Process

We started to smile as we read this section. After all, anyone involved in education at the K–12 level has experienced this issue: recess duty, playground duty, chaos duty! You can go anywhere in the country and see this over and over again. You choose the numbers: 50, 100, 200 kids in some abstractly defined space, and the keepers of the chaos—again choose the number—2, 5, 7 adults with different titles: teacher, aide, assistant, volunteer. Why is this done again and again across the country?

David's approach was to name the issue, provide some data, share the past, and tap the talents of his faculty to become effective problem solvers. In order to find a way out of the box of traditional thinking and solutions, David reframed the issue: What is the educational value of recess? Does recess improve student learning? Is it in our best interest to try to do something about this situation?

We are now beginning to see an important developmental thread with the first three issues that David tackled with his staff: The first issue, the faculty room, was a relatively low-risk, high-reward proposition for the faculty. They really didn't have anything to lose, and it did not impact any change in the instructional practices in the classroom. This event was really for them. The second issue, recess, shows some growth, because the faculty was willing to link the organizational solution with best instructional practice.

The third issue, the playground, went further to tie organizational solutions with improved programs for students. It would have been easy for teachers to have said, "We don't have to do recess duty" or "We only have to supervise recess five days a year" and let the issue continue. However, the teachers decided that the greater good was important enough to invest in a new process for problem solving. This professional behavior was novel for the faculty.

Building upon trust and a common vision, David saw his faculty demonstrate commitment. As a learning organization, this faculty is beginning to thrive. But a pessimistic eye can't help but notice that the planning period, the faculty room, and the recess issues minimally impacted teachers at the instructional classroom level. Is that why they were willing to work on these concerns?

DISCOVERING YOUR ADVOCATE

Many people assume than an advocate is a person with a particular passion for some vital cause. Advocates are most often associated with the legal system or with special interest groups. Our use of the Advocate as a metaphor actually expands the role and intention of advocacy to the domain of leadership and organizational development. The exemplars we've cited for the Advocate archetype provided unique perspectives about change agency and its relationship to leadership behavior and institutional growth.

In summary, we refer to leaders characterized by the Advocate archetype as exhibiting a strong commitment to a cause beyond oneself. Representative principals of this archetype viewed the school as a microcosm of a larger society. As instructional leaders, they believed all classroom learning must have practical application to community contexts to help students integrate concepts and understand their relevance to the real world. Advocate archetypes are particularly committed to those educational programs and instructional approaches that contribute to students' moral development and social consciousness.

When considering the descriptions and stories of leaders representing the Advocate archetype, what realizations about your own values and goals were inspired? Here are a series of additional questions you might want to ask yourself, based on this chapter's leadership archetype:

1. What are you willing to fight for? Is that part of the vision for your school or organization?

2. What causes are important for schools to address that provide meaningful lessons for students?

3. How successful have you been in reframing issues that address a cause beyond yourself?

4. What reframing and problem-solving strategies used by David would you consider applying to your context?

5. Is there a match between your core values and intrinsic beliefs and the issue of advocacy?

The answers to these questions require reflection and analysis through rational thinking. Although your responses might take some time to develop, ultimately you'll have shaped a reasonable and logical explanation for how you relate your professional experiences and beliefs to the Advocate archetype.

On the following pages, we've posed similar questions with tasks intended to stimulate your creative thinking. When you've completed the activities, we invite you to compare your responses from both the rational and the intuitive sides of your brain. We trust you'll not only identify unique perspectives but also arrive at a fuller and more holistic understanding of yourself as a leader and as an advocate.

REFLECTION QUESTIONS AND ACTIVITIES

Leadership Self-Assessment

1. Here are the ISLLC standards for school leaders that are being adopted by most states for certification of school administrators. (See Resource for more comprehensive descriptions.)

   ISLLC Standards

   I. The Vision of Learning

   II. The Culture of Teaching and Learning

   III. The Management of Learning

   IV. Relationships with the Broader Community to Foster Learning

   V. Integrity, Fairness, and Ethics in Learning

   VI. The Political, Social, Economic, Legal, and Cultural Context of Learning

   Which standards reflect the Gardener's expertise and weaknesses? How would you compare your ISLLC rating of the Gardener with yourself?

Leadership Assessment: Thinking Map Analysis

2. Think about the metaphor of the Gardener. On the next page is a **tree map** representing categories mentioned in "The Evolution of a Leadership Metaphor." Using the tree map (Hyerle, 1996), list issues you are faced with as a school leader.

Tree Map

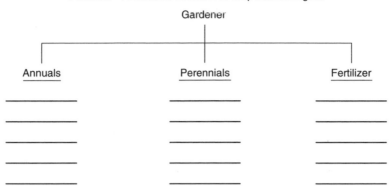

Annuals—Done or performed once a year every year
Perennials—Appearing again and again; recurrent
Fertilizer—Resources available to help initiatives grow

3. Look at the list. Highlight the issues that are related to being a manager of a school. Circle the items that address an instructional leader of a school. What do you notice?

4. How can you create systemic changes in your school by using fertilizer (resources) as an instructional leader through professional development?

5. Reflect on the core values of the Gardener. Can you identify them and apply them to his practice?

Organizational Assessment: Metaphoric Analysis

6. What are your core values, and how do they translate into your professional practice? Using the following **bridge map** (Hyerle, 1996), develop some insights about your core values and how they are actualized in your school.

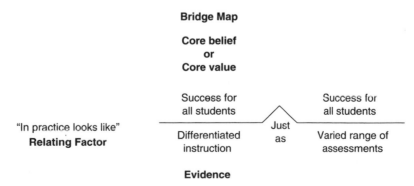

Bridge Map

Core belief
or
Core value

The way to read this map based on the example of the core value of *success for all students* would be

Success for all students "in practice looks like" differentiated instruction just as *success for all students* "in practice looks like" a varied range of assessments.

7. How many core values can you identify? Are you able to provide examples that translate your core values into the professional practices at your school?

The Parent

Everyone's Icon of Moral Leadership

The *Parent* archetype represents the leader who fashions and sustains a moral vision for the school that focuses on an ethic of care. This is the nurturer, or what Bolman and Deal would characterize as the human resource type, the leader who uses his or her administrative and interpersonal skills to develop and uphold positive community ideals by perpetuating strong school spirit, commitments to worthwhile causes, respect for individuality, diversity, and empowered students and staff. He or she values intimacy through close personal relationships he or she develops and takes particular pride in the accomplishments of those under his or her stewardship much as a parent would about a child.

A high school principal whose metaphor was the *Giving Tree*, a name taken from the book written by Shel Silverstein, attached the significance of the book to his professional commitment as a school leader. "To do for others is my calling," he says. He talks about four women in his life who helped nurture his core values of strong professional effort and personal sacrifice for others. "Within each," he added, "I viewed an aspect of myself that I would like to cultivate. Their stories, like those of countless other 'givers,' are stories I hope I may someday honor by imitation. I would also like to be thought of as a 'giver.'"

He is excited by the challenge of being a new leader in a school that historically struggles to meet state standards in a town where the community's support traditionally wavers. His goal is to inspire pride in the school and to reach out to students by developing an awareness and sensitivity to their issues. His leadership credo is based on the belief that listening to his student body will drive the actions he takes as the leader of this school.

His voice softens when he considers the influences on his understanding of leadership. "My mother instilled in me a level of caring that runs deep. She epitomized the Giving Tree." He thinks about the challenges that confront him and remains steadfast in his conviction to improve the quality and character of his school. "I like creating communities," he says with a smile. Then he heads off to an assembly to congratulate his juniors for their markedly improved scores on the recent state assessment.

Mufasa, a name inspired by the father of *The Lion King,* is how a middle school principal views himself as a leader. Originally hired as the assistant principal, he assumed the principalship four days prior to the opening of school. His goal, like that of the Giving Tree, was breaking down the barriers between administration and students. Sometimes this was done subtly by placing comfortable benches near the main office and by posting thought-provoking signs in the hallways.

"I never saw myself as a father figure," this principal confesses. "But a few years ago, when I was coaching, the team captain began calling me Mufasa. She even gave me a poster of the cartoon character." He sits back and reflects on his first year as principal and the metaphor he's adopted. "You know," he muses, "I have 440 kids in this building. I tell them often, once you're mine, you're mine."

The *Bridge* is a principal who came from the business sector. Education seemed a more comfortable fit with his desire to work in a collaborative community that develops common vision and thrives on teamwork. He boasts about the character and citizenship programs he's developed in the school.

"I'm a bridge," he says, "because I regard relationships as the key to learning and understanding. My job is to bridge the gaps of indifference, neglect, and distrust that get in the way of communication and working for the betterment of kids." Having grown up as a middle child in a family with four brothers, he learned early in life how to mediate conflict and create unity. "It's often what I do as a principal with both children and adults. Leadership is not a spectator sport. It means rolling up your sleeves, showing people you care, and being a hands-on administrator."

The *Daddy* is a high school principal who likes to talk about the traditions that characterize the relationships with students he's established in the school. His favorites are the Christmas dinners served by students to the faculty, the ice cream socials where teachers serve sundaes to students, or breakfasts the honor society makes for the staff. He reflects on his earlier experiences working with gangs in the Bedford Stuyvesant area of

Brooklyn, New York. "Something clicked back then," he says. "I realized my job was to make the world a better place."

He rises from his desk, walks over to a bookcase, takes a yearbook from one of the shelves, and reads aloud what former students wrote to him upon their graduation. "You showed compassion," one writes. Another calls him "friend." A third student talks about what the principal taught him about poetry and its relevance to world issues. "I'll never forget this student," the principal says. "It was during a class I was teaching that he just blurted out, 'Oh my god. I get it!' I actually observed his epiphany. And today, he's an environmentalist at a major university!"

He sits down again and reflects on his work in education, which spans three decades. "It's getting kids to be human and out in the world, to civilize them." He points to a picture of another student on his wall. "She's the nicest person I've met. She just lights it up. That's what the world needs."

Like the exemplar in Chapter 2, a number of principals identified themselves as a Gardener. One leader of an elementary school viewed each student as a plant that needs water, sunlight, and tender care to grow. "To make it all happen," she says, "I have to rely on a variety of skills: peacemaker, balancer, motivator, and nurturer."

She acknowledges that the roots of her garden began as a middle child in a devout Catholic family. "I was often the caretaker and mediator because our parents, while never letting us fight as kids, left it to us to figure out how to coexist. That's where I learned about shared decision making." She thinks about her background and the metaphor she's chosen for herself. "My staff is all part of this garden. They see me finding ways to encourage everyone's contribution to the development of the color and glory of our school."

Another elementary school principal referred to himself as a *Tolkach*. "It's an old term for 'fixer' that I discovered when I was studying Russian history," he stated. In pre-Soviet society, the *tolkachi* lived in rural villages and were responsible for getting things people needed. "'Let me see what I can do for you,'" he acknowledges, "is often what I hear myself saying to students, parents, and teachers, much like a Tolkach. That's my job as a leader: being part of a network for getting resources to help people."

Frequently during our discussions with principals, they acknowledged that their colleagues created metaphors for them. *The Guide by the Side* shunned the center stage as the leader of a middle school. "Never did I consciously go about being the Guide at the onset of my career," she admits. "Nor did I have any understanding of how important this style was to my success until many years into my first principalship. It was through the understanding of and great ability to observe me with people that one of my supervisors gave me this label."

She reflects on her role as a leader. This year she moved to a new middle school in the district she's been working in for quite some time. Her reputation as a supportive leader who believes in shared decision making preceded her. She's an avid cheerleader for her profession, who views her actions as caring and not as acts of control. "I like to help people do their job," she states matter-of-factly. "My job is to empower people to be their own leaders: to guide them in making sound decisions that work for students."

EXEMPLARS OF THE PARENT ARCHETYPE

The *Father of 1,453 Children Plus 2, With a Large Extended Family* best illustrates the Parent archetype. He models best instructional practices for student behavior by establishing a sense of community and respect throughout the school. He is neither aloof nor standoffish. He is willing to put himself on the line for students even at the expense of being dunked in a pool or duct-taped to a wall to raise money for meaningful causes.

This Father is not afraid to hold his students accountable to high moral standards. He understands the egocentric nature of adolescents and finds ways for them to think and feel beyond themselves by encouraging innovative fund-raisers, by leading pep rallies, by providing assemblies that offer experiences in appropriate public decorum, and by honoring accomplishment in all intellectual, athletic, social, vocational, and creative venues.

Consider how this Father cares about and respects his students and staff. He begins his community building by modeling acceptable and purposeful behaviors. Then he navigates the classrooms, hallways, cafeteria, and community sites to bring the school together. Finally, he empowers his teachers and students to instruct and lead among their own constituencies to integrate and disseminate the moral visions of respect, equity, and the ethic of care that characterize his school.

Then contrast the Father with David, who has arrived at the twilight of his tenure as principal. Consistent with his experiences at the school, a new challenge confronts him and the faculty during his last year as leader.

Once again, David reflects with his staff on the school's history of challenging issues and successful resolutions that sustained the school's moral purpose to advocate the best interests of children. This time, however, David takes a significant leap in moral leadership by working with both teachers and students to link the resolution of an organizational problem with the vision to advance student and school-community learning.

David's story in "The Giving Tree of a Second Kind" portrays a powerful model of problem reframing that dramatizes how adults and students can develop creative and proactive responses to address seemingly noneducational issues. This process successfully enhanced shared learning for all members of the school and fostered a positive approach to connecting organizational solutions with both the instructional and moral visions of the educational institution. Observe closely how this leader reacts to a crisis that can potentially threaten the stability and health of the school community. Through his efforts, David adeptly reframes the adults' and students' anticipated grieving to arrive at acceptance and emotional healing during the removal of two treasured 50-year-old trees sacrificed for a building addition project.

I AM THE FATHER OF 1,453 CHILDREN PLUS 2, WITH A LARGE EXTENDED FAMILY

by Bryan Lane

During the annual Spirit Week trivia competition the following question was asked: "How many children does our principal Mr. Lane have?" Without hesitation the sophomore class representative raised his hand first to respond, then answered in strong voice, "1,453." The sophomores were given ten points for a correct answer.

Being seen as a father to this many students may seem unrealistic to many. As a school administrator, I think about what I want from the parents of my students, and it comes down to some simple but very important things. These are the things that I think really make the difference when a student gets to high school.

1. The parent needs to set limits and stick to them. Whether there is one parent or two, this needs to be the norm, and one parent should not be able to be played off the other by the child.

2. The child should be introduced to the idea that there is something bigger than the child. This can be done through religious training or through the exposure to nature and the world around them, or both.

3. The child should be exposed to an extended family. This can be relatives or close friends who are like family.

4. The basic ideas of right and wrong should be shown to the child by consistent positive examples.

5. The idea that all children in a family are different and that there are things about them that make them special should be highlighted.

6. Adults should celebrate the child and be there as a hand to hold or a shoulder to cry on when he or she needs it.

This is exactly what we try to give our students at my school.

Setting Limits

In the movies or in real life, how many times have we heard the expression "my father will kill me if I get caught"?

When it comes down to it, my students know that most times if they do something silly they will get caught. It is a team effort from the entire staff, but it is important that the students see me as someone who is directly involved. The students see that I am visible, and they think that I am everywhere. I have even been accused of being cloned from time to time.

The students in my school know that there are standards for their behavior at all times, and they are strictly held to these standards. There are three basic rules that I have: (1) Students will respect themselves and others; (2) when a staff member tells a student to do something, the student will do what he or she is asked to do as long as it does not cause harm; (3) students will go to class and try their best on any given day. They know this because I tell them on the first day of school. I speak to them in groups and as individuals, and I continually preach these three things to them. I am in the halls and in the cafeteria regularly. I speak to students, and I call them on behaviors that may seem small, but these actions help to create the limits that we need to have in place. If a student is using inappropriate language in a conversation, you cannot just let it go because it is easier. It needs to be addressed. Warnings for most students work well because, basically, most of them are good kids. For those who don't heed the warnings, we cannot be afraid to discipline appropriately. The principal that lets things go only creates an environment that cannot be brought under control. It is my job as the principal to hold the line.

My head custodian called me on the two-way radio to let me know I needed to come to the bathroom by room 105 to look at something written on the wall. I asked him if it was written about me; he said yes. I then asked him if they had written "Lane" or "Mr. Lane." He let me know that it was "Mr. Lane," followed by something that was probably physiologically impossible. My response to him was, "They wrote it with respect; just take it off the wall."

I stopped taking things like that personally a long time ago. If a student writes my name on the wall instead of blowing up at a teacher or responding negatively to another student, I'm willing to take the heat. In dealing with students in disciplinary matters, it is essential to be consistent and fair, just as we hope most parents do. Playing favorites, as easy as it would be, is not the way to go. The students who have a consistent problem will have respect for us if we are consistent in our policies even if they don't like it. One of the best compliments I've received came from a young man who said, "I don't like him because he is a hard ass, but he is fair." I will take that one any day.

The World Is Bigger Than the Student

This is a tough one, not only because it depends on the principal's ability to have an effect on students but also because it must be the philosophy of the staff as a whole. Kids are easy; adults can often be the problem. Teenagers by their very nature are self-centered. They believe that they are invincible and that everyone else exists to recognize their needs and then provide for them. This is where the respect for self and others is the key. With the lead of the principal, each staff member must be looking beyond the needs of their class to the needs of the school as a whole. If the students see the principal as someone who looks out for others and who is willing to be vulnerable, they are more likely to follow that example.

Annually I spend two hours in the dunking booth at Old Home Days. This town fair has been going on for years, but my presence has become an expectation. For my students to see me out there willing to be silly and ready to risk being dunked by them is a great message. Spirit Week is one of my favorite times of the year. We have developed a scholarship fund from pennies, nickels, and dimes collected in a competition I call the Penny Exchange. Two years ago, I allowed any student who put a penny or more into the collection to have a four-foot piece of duct tape to be used to tape me to the wall. I stood on a platform for two hours during all lunches to orchestrate this event. Students were enthralled by the idea that collectively they could tape me to the wall. The goal behind this was to bring them together for a common purpose, and I was the bait. At the end of the two hours the platform was removed, and the tape held me to the wall; it was great. To this day students still talk about that as a great time together.

Finding things that bring the school community together is key, and the principal needs to be there to make sure that it can happen. Finding things and setting out the bait is my job. It took three years and a bunch of hand-holding to get the Key Club to buy into doing the Senior Citizens Prom, but now they have embraced it, and it has become a highlight for their year, not to mention a great community relations piece. It took four years to get the Future Farmers of America and the senior class to work together to do a "haunted hayride" at Halloween for a fund-raiser. It is now an annual event that people have come to enjoy, and the kids have been able to use our resources to provide a service to the community at large. The principal needs to be the guiding hand that not only allows things to happen but makes them happen as well. These activities, while they may be used as fund-raisers or other community relations, have the real purpose of bringing students together in a sense of community. This will build relationships among students and create a better atmosphere for your school. As a side note, it is always better to allow someone else to take the credit for these things, but everyone will eventually know that it is you behind the scenes allowing things to happen.

The principal must find a way to communicate this vision of the greater good to the staff. It is easy for teachers, who are often isolated in their classrooms, to only be concerned about what happens in their room. They work hard to find ways to help their students, and they sometimes forget that they are not alone. Whether it is in schoolwide initiatives that bring a focus to the efforts of the building or the small act of standing outside the classroom to greet and monitor students, the principal must work to make these things happen. The students will then see that there is a need to work together to be most effective. Just as parents have a network of other parents looking out for their children, the staff is the principal's network to look out for the greater good.

Exposure to an Extended Family

My wife and I had our second child in July while we were living in Texas. My father-in-law did not meet his granddaughter until Christmas. Such a distant relationship with family was not acceptable to us, so we decided to move back to New England; it was important to us that our children know that our family was more than just my wife and me. The extended family gives people the knowledge that there are those willing to support them even outside their immediate family circle. This gives children a sense of security in knowing that there are many who care for them. Growing up, I knew that if I did something I shouldn't, there were at least six neighbors who would either stop me or call the house to let my mom know what I had done. While I did not appreciate it at the time, I know now that these people were looking out for me so that I did not follow the wrong path.

I see myself as the patriarch of this huge school family. All students need to know that, while I will set limits, I do care about what happens to them. At first, this cannot be done by the principal alone. I need to create the atmosphere of family in the sense that each staff person is looking out for the students so that they do not go down the wrong path. To accomplish this, one needs to hire the right people and express an expectation for them that, while they are primarily responsible for teaching the students, they are also expected to look out for them. The development of my role on a one-to-one basis takes time. When the opportunity presents itself, students need to see me as the one who makes things happen.

I am the head cheerleader. I run each pep rally, I lead them in cheers, and the sight of me evokes emotion. They may not like the limits we set or the rules we enforce, but if they can see the passion in what we do, they can respect those limits and rules. No one can act with passion if he or she does not care. It is also important to make sure the staff knows that I care about them as I do the students. On schoolwide issues, although I create the inertia for change, it is always a good move to give credit for the positive things happening to staff members. This will give those who put in extra effort the desire to continue working toward new goals and, it is hoped, stimulate those who are hesitant to get involved. Giving the staff ownership of the process creates opportunities for the staff to really buy into what the principal is looking for. If each teacher, secretary, custodian, and aide can show the passion for what he or she does, the students are going to know that this large extended family cares for them.

A difficult part of this process is to get the students to care about each other. Many of them have built relationships before they arrive at my door. Some of these relationships are good, and others are full of ill will from the past. My first statement to them as a group of freshmen is that it does not matter where they have come from; they are all Broncos now. I try to use our mascot to symbolize what we do together. This comes back to the idea of there being something greater than themselves. If they can see that we are a community, then we are well on our way.

Each person must be treated with the same respect and dignity because all need to feel that they are equal. This is easier to do with a graduating class, but schoolwide issues can be used as well. In times of tragedy, a student body can split or come together as a large family to support each other. The tragedy of September 11, 2001, had the effect of bringing our students together because we gave them opportunities to show they cared. We made a sign to send to Ground Zero to thank the workers, we had a drive to gather food for the volunteers, and we had a lap-a-thon around the track to raise money for the Red Cross. All of these things brought us together and supported us collectively. My job was to make sure that those who had a need had the power to get things done. In these cases, it did not matter who got the credit for things; it was my job to build the capacity for leadership that brought people to the next level. This sense of community can be done by creating traditions that help the community and bring pride to our large family. Activities that bring community members together build a stronger community and create an even larger extended family and support system for students.

Right and Wrong

This sounds easier than it is. The problem is that different people have different perceptions of what is right and what is wrong. As my generation grew up, we played after school with kids in the neighborhood and we made up our own games. We had to develop the skills of debate, compromise, and resolution to make rules and then implement them. Today's students have been scheduled into soccer, gymnastics, after-school day care, and a myriad of other things where adults make up all the rules. The social behaviors that we expect our students to have mastered have not been practiced, because in many cases they have not been given the opportunity to master them. It has become our job to give the students these experiences whether we want to or not.

In determining how the ideas of right and wrong are implemented, the principal must lead by example without question. We are not allowed to have bad days, to say the wrong thing, or to do something that does not follow the perception of right and wrong. If I am at a function where my students are present, I will not have a social drink even though my superintendent may choose to do so. During the school day, I wear a tie no matter how hot it is. If I am in a store in the community I will always say please and thank you to the attendant at the store. If I am walking down the hallway and see a piece of paper on the floor, I will always pick it up. These may seem like small things, but they are the things that make a difference.

Students need to be shown what is right and what is wrong because many times they do not know subtle differences. If the principal does not create opportunities for assemblies, how are students going to know how to behave in a public setting? When I arrived at my school, there hadn't been a pep rally in years; they did not know how to cheer. We fight with reality television shows each day, not to mention daily news coverage of violence and abuse, to provide more compelling and less sensational ways to consider what is right and what is wrong.

The looser our society becomes, the harder it is for us to fight the idea of what is acceptable in our schools. We cannot lower our expectations for right and wrong. The student code of conduct should be made to guide students, and students should have input into what is considered to be right and wrong. If there is a dress code, the students should have a voice. This does not mean that the principal abdicates the decision, but any good leader will use the voices of those around him or her to make good decisions and recommendations.

The next step is to get the staff onboard. They have as many different views as the students do. There has to be consistency in what we are doing so that the students have an established path to follow. The staff need to understand that, although they may not be in total agreement with each specific item, they need to work together. Just as parents do not allow the child to play his or her needs off each parent, teachers cannot give the students the opportunity to play teachers off each other. This is where the principal must set the example of doing things the right way and insisting that the staff work together. Inasmuch as we set limits and standards for students, teachers must also be held accountable.

The final step is when the students start to teach each other what is right and what is wrong. If I have done my job well, my upper-classmen will lead by example and show freshmen that certain behaviors are "not cool." This needs to be done with respect and without hazing. A good example of this is that we no longer have a cigarette smoking problem in our school. While we have made sure that we hold the line on disciplinary action, the students have policed themselves, because they don't like the smoke in the bathrooms either. When principals develop this leadership in their students, they are ready to go out on their own.

What happens when the principal has a bad day? Without question the principal needs to acknowledge this. If the bad day manifests in behavior directed at a specific student, an apology is due. If a series of days go by when there has been some general "grumpiness" to staff and students, the apology should be made to the school as a whole. This should be rare, but if it is done with humility and sincerity, you will gain more than you lose.

Treating Each Person as an Individual

It is important for parents to look at the special things that make each child different. The old Smothers Brothers routine that insisted, "Mom liked you best," is not something that really works when raising children. For the principal, there are two arenas where this comes into play. The first is when two students are siblings. Sometimes students in the same family have similar characteristics and tend to have equal levels of success. This is not usually true. Being compared to a sibling is unfair. If the sibling was not academically focused and had difficulty in dealing with school rules, it is not fair to assume that the younger sibling will have the same problems. While many times the home environment can create similar problems, we cannot come to a conclusion in advance that the student will have the same problems or react to the new school environment in the same way. The converse of this is the expectation that because one student did well, so will a younger brother or sister. Living in someone's shadow is never easy, and comparisons of siblings at school should never be made.

The other arena is cliques and stereotyping. Some of the nicest kids I have ever met have had green hair and pierced eyebrows or tongues. While I am relieved that this is not my child leaving the house like that, it must be acknowledged that these individuals are often very creative and good students. It is never acceptable to look at students who dress in black, or back in the early 1990s in the grunge style, and assume that they will be trouble. The principal must lead the charge for equal treatment.

Many times there is an assumption that athletes are treated differently from others. In my school, I do treat athletes differently: I expect more from them. If they choose to wear the uniform, they represent me and every other person involved in the school. I need these students to lead by ensuring that others are treated with respect. If not, they forfeit the privilege of wearing the uniform. There is also the perception by some that students involved in vocational programs are less academically motivated than others. Our school is also a regional vocational technical center. This means we have 13 vocational programs in our building with more than 60 percent of our students involved in one or more of these programs daily. It has become part of our school culture that these programs are important and have rigor that will challenge each student. The principal must create the atmosphere in which all of these students are valued for their efforts.

I would challenge any student who can earn an A in calculus to try to play an instrument, paint a portrait, repair a carburetor, climb a tree carrying a chain saw, work with animals, perform an oration from Shakespeare, plan a lesson for a class of three-year-olds, cook a meal for a crowded restaurant, be a bank teller, grow a crop of corn, or sing a solo. I am proud to say that these are all things that happen in our school daily. All of our students need to be appreciated and honored for their individual accomplishments.

Celebrating and Support

The principal is supposed to know everything that happens in the building. While that is not possible, it is important to know the things that are going well and those things that are causing difficulty. Celebrating something that someone does sounds easy, but the trick is not to leave anyone out. If the football team wins on Friday night, is that any less important than the woodsman team winning at the county fair or the robotics team winning at a local competition? The answer must be no, they are all of equal value. Getting the information so that students can be recognized is not always simple. A system of communication needs to be in place so that this information gets to the principal.

Celebrating can be done in many ways. The state of New Hampshire recognizes seniors who are scholar athletes in separate ceremonies for boys and girls. The first year I went to the ceremony and did not make a big deal of it was a mistake. This is a significant accomplishment. Every year since then I have celebrated this in a unique way. I have rented a limousine to drive the award winners to the ceremony and then out to lunch with me. This may sound extravagant. A school bus for five hours would cost around $200. The limousine company has charged me $250 for the same amount of time. For $50 more I have found a way to give these young people a treat to remember. The way I figure it, if all those who were recognized bought one soda per week over their four years at my school from the soda machine, they actually paid for it themselves.

Every year I sit down on a Saturday in the fall and call each freshman who makes the honor roll in the first quarter. It takes about four to six hours over the weekend, but it really makes a difference to these students and their parents. At the end of each school year, I write a card to seniors who have distinguished themselves or have gone through a struggle and made it to the graduation stand. It takes time, but they really remember. I have a Bronco Pin program. I give out Pride Pins to students who do good things. They do not have to be athletes or top students. These are students who do things for others because it is who they are.

The biggest way that I choose to celebrate my students is by getting to know them. I take the time to watch and listen to them. I look for the things they do that make them special, and I find a time to let them know how I feel about them. These are the things that people remember, and they help me as well through days that are not always easy.

The hardest thing I have ever had to do was tell a young man that his mother had died. They don't teach you this one in any of the graduate classes on school leadership. I am a firm believer that I will not ask anyone else to do something that I wouldn't do. How could I have asked anyone else to deliver such a message? Death is handled in many different ways. I have been to 29 funerals of students that I have had, some while they were in school and some after they had graduated. I have been to a countless number of parent funerals as well as staff funerals. My job is to be there for my students and staff. It is up to me to offer a presence that gives them someone to turn to when they feel that there is no one else. I almost always stand so that my students can see where I am. At the church I am in the back watching to see if anyone needs help. At the cemetery I stand behind the students because they know that I am always behind them in support. I first understood that when a student I thought was not fond of me came up to me at a funeral and hugged me. He would not let go, and he finally started to cry, which I knew was what he needed. We never spoke of it again, but every time he looked at me thereafter it was as if he was saying thank you. It still touches me today when I think about it.

The other things that happen in a student's life, whether it is being dumped by a boyfriend or girlfriend, parents divorcing, dealing with substance abuse issues, failing a test, or not graduating, are issues I've had to address each year. My job is to make sure students are given resources to find their way. If that means you go to bat for a student who did not get a homework assignment done or needs more time to study, you do that. His or her teacher will not always agree, but if you have held the line on other things that have supported teachers, they will at least know your motives are good. Someday that teacher may need the same kind of consideration.

Grades 9 to 12 are times that are full of change, and they are scary. I am in the parking lot every morning so that I can watch my students come in. I can see who is in a good mood, who is not with whom, or who seems troubled. I am in the halls during passing time and the cafeteria whenever possible. These are all times to get to know students and to let them get to know you. If you can spot them when they are in trouble and intercede, they will always remember.

A good teacher is a good storyteller. My teaching has moved out of the classroom and into the realm of real life. Most times I can come up with a story or anecdote appropriate to a student's situation and show him or her that there is light at the end of the tunnel. It comes from knowing yourself and knowing your kids.

The real success to being a father to all of my children comes from taking the time to get to know them. The Breaking Ranks II research that has just come out speaks about personalizing your school. The successful principal fosters an environment where all staff members can develop relationships with students, but it is important that the one who works the hardest at that is the principal.

REFLECTIONS ON THE FATHER

The father of 1,453 kids plus 2, with a large extended family. Talk about responsibility! Talk about meeting needs! Talk about leadership!

When we think of our own extended family and observe this Father, our emotions awaken to feelings of security and love, memories of what we experienced as children, the importance of family rituals and traditions, and the breaking of bread—sharing a meal as a family unit.

The Father's story illustrates an unwritten obligation to provide, in this case, for the members of his school. As a parent, this leader seems to have an intuitive sense of his school's purpose and what his kids are about. Curiously, one word the Father never discussed in his essay was *trust.* Yet it's one of the most important traits that define him as a leader.

The Father builds and capitalizes on trust in some traditional and meaningful ways: he lectures students, he shares bits of wisdom with his teachers, he sets expectations for the adults and the youth. With this foundation of trust, the Father perpetuates a vision characterized by seven core beliefs. We've reframed these beliefs from the students' and teachers' perspectives and developed guiding questions for each principle. As an example of the Parent archetype, these beliefs are underscored by an ethic of care, a desire to encourage adults and children to contribute to the larger society, and a wish to provide opportunities for all members of the school to respect the potential they possess as humans as they seek to uncover and reveal their hidden talents.

1.   Core belief: Setting limits and being consistent help students make wise and responsible decisions.

Guiding question for students: What are my limits?

"When you are in my house, you are going to live by my rules!" This phrase has been echoed by fathers throughout generations. In this story, Brian (the principal) begins by communicating his beliefs to students and teachers on the first day of school. Brian, the Father, does this in a firm and caring way, not as a dictator.

2.   Core belief: There are acceptable and unacceptable behaviors that people must understand in a conscious community.

Guiding question for students: What is right, what is wrong, and why?

Notice how Brian *overcommunicates* his ideals. He lives by them. He models respectful behaviors, and he supports students and teachers who do the same by holding everyone accountable to the community ethos. As a Parent archetype, Brian communicates an ethic of care that forms the foundation of a conscious community. "All of these children are ours, and even though each one is unique, we must provide a safe and fair environment for each of us. This is how we build respect. This allows us to be consistent. It doesn't matter what stage we are in life; when we are aware of our limits, we feel safe knowing that there is an expectation of behaviors and actions that allows us to function as a group. Once the boundaries are established, rules of behavior follow. Each of us must understand the difference between 'right' and 'wrong.'"

Brian is not an idealist. He understands the complexities of creating a school culture: "This sounds easier than it is." He communicates without sounding pompous or morally superior.

Like a good parent, Brian leads without personalizing issues or behaving reactively to apparent criticism. The "bathroom graffiti incident" makes us chuckle: "I then asked him if they had written 'Lane' or 'Mr. Lane.'" He understands adolescents and their impulsive nature to strike out at authority when frustrated, anxious, or angry. Brian knows which battles to take on. He knows if it's a pattern of concern or an act of disillusionment. He also knows that in the face of criticism, he is the adult. That means withholding judgment and viewing a student's frustration by focusing on the big picture. How would the bathroom wall event be resolved in your school? Would the custodian agree with Brian's response? This principal teaches, models, applies knowledge, and provides opportunity for students and all staff, even the custodians, to act with wisdom and concern for the people they serve and with whom they work.

3. Core belief: As members of a school, we are a supportive community, much like an extended family.

Guiding question for students: Who cares?

"Who cares?" That statement reflects Brian's response to a student, a teacher, or an attitude. He starts off with, *"I care!"* and then demonstrates his commitment through actions, not words alone.

There is a fundamental shift that must penetrate the ways schools operate today if we want to adapt what Brian is trying to do in his school community. Brian shows that he cares by being passionate, by cheering, by supporting, and by unifying. After all, "it does not matter where you came from; we are all Broncos now!"

4. Core belief: I am not you, and that's OK. You are not me, and that's OK. Let's support each other.

Guiding question for students: Who am I? Who are you?

Who am I? Being the father of 1,453 + 2 is an amazing concept. How does he even remember his students' names? Brian is committed to all children and adults finding their identities as students and teachers and, for all of them, as learners. He talks about the need to challenge cliques and stereotypes. There are the "jock" and the "geek," the "vo-tech" and the "artsy."

Brain reflects on his environment and says, "Yes, this is who we are! Isn't it great?" He observes differences but is not judgmental. He sees potential. He attacks the barriers of narrow thinking by challenging students and teachers to get out of their comfort zones. A powerful way to do that is through empathy. Try playing an instrument, try repairing a carburetor, try playing a sport. As an educational leader, Brian demands rigor in his curriculum. He wants the teachers and students engaged in meaningful work where talents are valued. He creates a culture where students can determine who they want to be and be proud of who they are becoming.

5. Core belief: The school is a microcosm of society. The world is larger than the student.

Guiding question for students: What are my place and responsibility in the world?

Brian understands that, as students are trying to figure out who they are, they are also beginning to question their place in the world and where they fit in it. Brian's intuition about kids leads him to consider what's going on inside the hearts and minds of his students and how their internal search for meaning is reflected in the school and community.

How often in education does it seem that the only time we ask students to be a part of something bigger than ourselves is when a major tragedy has occurred? In schools following September 11, 2001, or the more recent tsunami crisis, we encouraged this need to connect, this need to help. But when it comes to smaller issues, we witness apathy. On some levels, students continue to ask, "How does this impact me? Why should I care?" Brian addresses these questions by finding local issues on which to focus student attention and reflection. As an instructional leader, he pushes his community to apply what they are learning in the classroom to real-world problems.

Brian knows that school culture is a part of a larger community, so he explores resources and causes that can bring the two together. First he reveals his ethic of care and his passion by taking a risk—being vulnerable—by doing things because they're good things to do. In Brian's own words, "It took three years to . . . " and "It took four years to. . . ": What's the message he's sending? This is important to me, I care, this is our community, and we are all a part of it.

Some of the events Brian creates require careful orchestration, which demonstrates his sensitivity and understanding of the school's vulnerability to the whims and pressures of the outside community. His response? He selects achievable challenges with built-in success. Have students host a Senior Citizens Prom! How might those seniors vote now at budget time?

Another goal inherent in Brian's vision is developing future leaders. If students have more understanding and awareness of who they are and how they are connected to the larger society, won't they in turn bring these principles to their work, their school, and their community? This is fundamental to Brian's intrinsic beliefs about school leadership.

6.   Core belief: The school is where I can find support for growth as a student and as a teacher.

Guiding question for students: Who can help?

Brian recognizes his school is a community designed for young people to grow, examine, and discover. There is a day when students will move on from school and, like a father, Brian understands that his role is both developmental and transitory. While my 1,453 + 2 kids are here, they need to fail, they need to ask for help, they need to know that people care, and they need to see purpose. He creates an environment where faculty and students know support is always accessible. Sometimes it's through talking, sometimes it's through listening, and sometimes it's just letting a student know he's there.

Brian's ethic of care spirals and overlaps. In order to ask for help, you must show vulnerability. In order to get support, someone has to care. In order to care, you have to understand the rules and the limits. It's a natural interaction that creates a thriving culture.

7.   Core belief: Each of us has special talents worthy of recognition, respect, and celebration.

Guiding question for students: Why should I feel proud?

Ask kids today what they are proud of. They might react with a blank stare or a shoulder shrug or might possibly mention something that happened outside of school. Brian teaches what it means to be proud in school, and he celebrates it openly. Pride pins make someone feel special. Overcoming great challenges through effort and work is valued. How does Brian project this understanding? He looks for it and finds examples to proclaim. He gets to know his students by finding that which makes them special, and he broadcasts their worth, their skills, and their uniqueness as individuals to the school community.

Whenever we see a baby take a step for the first time we cheer, hoot, and holler! As a leader, Brian challenges all of us to look at the children in our schools today and find cause to applaud and celebrate their achievements. He's a very proud father who revels in the accomplishments of his children.

There is a time as children when each of us has wondered about our parents: "After you're gone, who is going to take care of us?" Brian reassures his students that they have the strength, the talents, and the skills to carry on.

The idea of leadership as a conceptual construct for family in a school environment is not new. "In loco parentis" (literally, in the place of a parent) is a well-worn phrase that has characterized the function of schools in America. Brian's leadership represents a focus on creating "intimate" relationships with his students and staff through the power of intention. He knows when to speak and when to take corrective action. He knows when to allow a student to struggle and when to be supportive.

Support comes in many forms. Sometimes it means Dad as the funny guy—getting dunked in a pool or taped to a wall. But it's even deeper than that, because both of those examples were for a greater cause, not a bribe to do better on a test but a sincere form of fun to benefit someone else. Support can also be seen through silence—just knowing that Dad is there, knowing that he cared enough to be a part of something without having to be the center of it.

Brian raises an interesting question. Doesn't every school need a father of its children as its leader? It's not the trophy or the laudatory press release that leaves a lasting impression on students and teachers at Brian's school. Really, it's about a leader who shows every day that he cares deeply and passionately about every individual that walks the halls of his school. That's what students and teachers will remember most about the father of 1,453 children plus 2.

DAVID'S EVOLUTION AS A LEADER, PART 3: THE GIVING TREE OF A SECOND KIND

We've now come to the end of David's last year as principal of the school. His anticipated retirement, coupled with the construction of a new gym and multipurpose room, marked a significant transition for the school. While everyone from teachers to students and community members were delighted with the prospect of a new space for physical education and drama productions, there was only one problem. The 50-year-old trees behind the school would have to be taken down.

Once again, David tried to find a creative solution to this problem. The trees were part of the playground community for students. They provided shade and special places where students could sit and read or visit in small groups. Often during the warm-weather days in June, teachers would bring their classes outside and provide instruction under the canopy of the trees.

The silver maples had grown to more than forty feet and provided hues of crimson and bright orange during the fall and emerald greens in spring each year. David and the teachers tried to persuade the school board and the architect to find another location for the addition or to change its placement so the trees could remain. But their proposals were denied, and when the building project began in March, David knew there would be much grieving about the trees.

At a faculty meeting to discuss the issue, David listened to the teachers' concerns. "We're upset, and we know the children will be too," one teacher complained. "It's a bad situation. And there's nothing we can do!"

David reminded teachers how they had adopted proactive approaches to remedy past issues at school. He reviewed their commitment to linking organizational and building-related solutions to improved student learning. "So what are some of the lessons we want children to learn from this experience?" he asked.

Immediately, teachers began to suggest a variety of activities that students could engage in to commemorate the trees. But David held up his hands and stopped the discussion. "We're jumping the gun," he said. "Like all good planning for instruction, we need to start by identifying a process that addresses our community grieving, and we can't do that without first establishing the overarching standards and big ideas that characterize the learning experiences we want for the children and the adults at our school."

As they had in past faculty meetings, everyone understood and accepted the process David proposed. Drawing a large circle map to elicit learning standards, David guided the faculty in creating four conceptual statements:

1. Students will understand that change is inevitable and can be both positive and negative.

2. Students will understand that historical traditions and nature are important to people.

3. Students will understand that living a positive life means finding good in everything.

4. Students will understand that if people take away from nature, they must find ways to give back and to honor nature.

The following day, the four standards were posted in the faculty room and distributed to all teachers to discuss with students in preparation for the removal of the trees. During classroom discussions, children were encouraged to name one big idea for each standard. By the end of the week, David convened another faculty meeting to refine and edit the student ideas. They identified the following four:

1. All living things adapt to change.

2. People respect trees because they are an important part of our environment and contribute to our well-being.

3. Losing our trees and a section of our playground will give our school a new gym.

4. People renew our environment when it has been damaged or destroyed.

During the next week, the standards and big ideas were reviewed with each class. Now students were asked to consider possible activities the school could observe to honor the trees and to accept their sacrifice for a new gym space. This is what they said:

For Standard and Big Idea 1:

1. Brainstorm changes we've all had to make and how we dealt with them in positive ways.

2. Create sculptures out of the tree trunks for the playground.

3. Use the tree stumps for playground tables and seats.

4. Donate the trees to families who heat their homes with wood.

For Standard and Big Idea 2:

1. Post thank-you wishes to the trees.

2. Research possible uses of silver maples.

3. Interview the past principal of the school who was here 30 years ago about the history of the trees, and create a plaque in his or her honor.

4. Have classes read books about trees, write and illustrate stories about trees, and display them.

5. Have the sixth graders conduct a mock trial about the trees coming down.

6. Stage a simulated sit-in protest about the trees, and connect the issue to events in U.S. history.

For Standard and Big Idea 3:

1. Create compare and contrast posters showing what the school is giving up and what the school is getting.

2. Cut wood cookies from each trunk and mark the tree rings with important events that occurred in the town's and the nation's history.

3. Read *The Giving Tree* by Shel Silverstein to the school.

4. Take bark rubbings of the tree and display them.

5. Have recess science lessons about rings of trees, core samples, and tree types.

For Standard and Big Idea 4:

1. Have a planting ceremony for two new trees.

2. Make benches out of the trees and locate them in the school lobby.

3. Take cuttings from the trees, and start and plant them on the playground.

4. Wear ribbons the week the trees come down.

On the final day of every year at David's school, a special rite of passage assembly honored the graduating sixth graders who would attend the middle school in the fall. Candles were distributed to them and to the fifth graders who stood facing them. All of the other students watched with their teachers and with invited parents and community members as the lights were dimmed and the sixth graders' candles were lit.

David approached the microphone and gazed out at the students and the audience. He began his description of the meaning of rites of passage and reflected on the contributions made by the oldest students to their school community. That year, he commended them for their reading of *The Giving Tree* in front of the trees behind the school the day before they were taken down. When he was finished with his speech, he instructed the sixth graders to light the candles of the fifth graders and concluded the assembly and his final day with students with this passing of the light.

David's journey as a principal represents one example of an instructional leader's development. His ability to build a cohesive culture over time required conviction and perseverance, vision and clarity, and humility in oneself and trust in others. His gift as an able administrator lies in the creative use of reflection and reframing to help him and others consider perspectives that address challenging obstacles to school and organizational success.

At his last faculty meeting, David reflected on his tenure at the school and his journey as a leader. "Looking back," he said, "what began for me as personal tragedy 35 years ago evolved into a journey about my healing and my awakening. My loss of eyesight represented a metaphor for needing to look at who I was through another set of lenses." Wiping away a tear, he continued, "Reframing helped me see what I was not paying attention to in my life and my work. Reframing enhanced my personal growth. It taught me about 'dis-ease' in a new way and introduced me to the negative view characterized by the victim mythology in my life and in the culture of our school."

In his journal that evening, David wrote, "Our wonderful rite of passage for the trees brought full circle my own rite of passage as a school leader to find the good in our obstacles and trust our innate creative wisdom as a faculty to discover positive solutions for challenging problems."

REFLECTIONS ON DAVID AND THE TREES

Stage 4 of Reframing: Renorming the Organization's Behavior

Given the episode with the removal of the trees at David's school, it appears that the framework for basing the impact of organizational decisions on improved student learning has become actualized. Now we see that a problem or challenge once again faces the school community at large. The emotionally charged issue was respected, but David grounded the faculty in the educational potential of this event and the process by which action could be taken.

The evidence of the development of standards, big ideas, and student activities provides impressive documentation that this organization has continued to grow in a healthy way with a passion for improved student learning. By using an outcome-based approach, the faculty developed essential questions. Students were also an integral part of the process through their development of the "big ideas" that were important to them. All of this was grounded in curriculum standards to create a transformational experience for the whole school.

We do not use the word *transformational* lightly here. We wondered as we read about David's journey if a higher standard of performance could be achieved by a faculty with a penchant for the victim mythology. Over the course of 18 years, David built trust, established a common framework, created a level of commitment, and had the capacity to obtain measurable results. The teachers are now making changes that impact their daily lives at the operational level. The issue about the trees having to be removed for the construction of a new gym informed instruction. It changed what was happening in the classroom. It penetrated all grade levels and all content areas. It removed in dramatic fashion the victim mythology and replaced it with a culture of heroines and heroes.

David's use of metaphor to describe the district's long-standing behavior served to catalyze the staff into a new frame of mind. This reframing or paradigm shift galvanized the teachers and created a shared experience from a new and provocative dimension of thinking and action.

By committing to a solution that was grounded in a program-driven recommendation, David and the faculty discovered another way to view problems. In the past, they had considered conflict as an obstacle to positive change. Now they observed the phenomenon of using problems to enhance the development and continuation of best instructional practices. As a result of this creative, outside-the-box strategy, the faculty and the principal reached a higher and more satisfying level of organizational development that became a permanent theme for subsequent planning and decision making.

David's ability to rely on reframing created solutions to a constellation of issues he and the staff were attempting to resolve. "Recreation education" became a new metaphor for how both children and adults viewed recess. By designing age-appropriate activities that were curriculum related, students were able to apply ideas in a variety of creative and engaging contexts.

Reframing was accepted as an effective tool for problem solving and decision making at David's school. Addressing issues by shifting people's consciousness led to creating new perspectives that in turn enhanced innovative and empowering solutions. Reframing also remained steadfast to the ideals and values reflected in the faculty's goal of working for what was in the best interests of children and adults.

Reframing evolves as a change process beginning with informing and storming of ideas, norming of values and goals, and performing in alignment with the school's vision and mission. Reframing as a tool for instructional leaders like David meant developing a school culture that valued divergent thinking to create programs and processes that resonated with instructional standards and best practices.

DISCOVERING YOUR PARENT

What kind of parents to students were your elementary or high school principals? Were they caring and attentive, committed to knowing their students by name and interests? Could they converse with students about issues other than school matters? Were they emotionally supportive, sometimes offering a hug or a pat on the back? Or were your former principals aloof, standoffish, and preoccupied with managing the school? Did they console compassionately or discipline authoritatively? How did they interact and communicate with you and your peers?

To summarize, the Parent archetype is committed to an ethic of care. We were surprised by the number of leaders who viewed themselves as the Parent of their school, particularly high school principals. They lead with compassion and believe that, by providing personal support, they more effectively enhance student learning and adult professional development. Principals of the Parent archetype thrive on close relationships with students, their families, and colleagues. They use the respect of their office to convey strong and sincere messages about the worth of each person in the school. Their primary goal is to help every person realize as much of his or her potential as possible.

In what ways do you transmit an ethic of care in your school or organization? Consider the following questions about your role and behavior as a leader from the perspective of the Parent archetype:

1. How well do you know your students and your staff?

2. What kinds of conversations and levels of intimacy do you have with students and staff beyond issues about school?

3. Compare and contrast your core values with the Parent archetype characteristics. What do you notice?

4. How do you convey compassion and caring to students and teachers?

5. If students from your school were asked if they perceived you as the school's parent, what do you imagine they would say?

Having concluded our discussion of the three leadership archetypes in the first section of this book, we now focus our attention on a more thorough understanding of reframing through metaphor. We'll begin in Chapter 4 by explaining the evolution of our thinking in light of contemporary writers on school leadership. In Chapter 5, we'll close by describing a variety of useful techniques that promote effective and imaginative organizational change.

REFLECTION QUESTIONS AND ACTIVITIES

Leadership Self-Assessment

1. Here are the ISLLC standards for school leaders that are being adopted by most states for certification of school administrators. (See Resource for more comprehensive descriptions.)

ISLLC Standards

   I. The Vision of Learning

  II. The Culture of Teaching and Learning

 III. The Management of Learning

 IV. Relationships with the Broader Community to Foster Learning

  V. Integrity, Fairness, and Ethics in Learning

 VI. The Political, Social, Economic, Legal, and Cultural Context of Learning

Based on the standards, which ones reflect the Parent's expertise and weaknesses? How would you compare your ISLLC rating of the Parent with yourself?

Leadership Assessment: Instructional Frame Analysis

Here are nine characteristics of an **Instructional** Leader:

- I model best teaching practices.
- I encourage reflection as part of the learning and teaching process.
- I communicate to staff, students, and parents best instructional practices.
- I understand child, adolescent, and adult learning theories.
- I espouse a school mission that supports a learning theory.
- I encourage applied academic learning to community contexts.
- I seek to broaden the instructional repertoire of teachers.
- I use assessment to evaluate curriculum and staff development.
- I use technology as a tool to improve instruction and higher order thinking.

2. Put a "+" symbol next to each characteristic that describes your everyday practice. It should be a trait that you have so well established that you could demonstrate its effectiveness to other leaders. Put an N next to each characteristic that you feel you need more work on in the way of professional development, coursework, or dialogue.

3. Reflect on being an instructional leader. How do you pull the pendulum back to create balance between the management of a school and the instructional leadership of a school? **Look back** at the nine characteristics. Look at the "+" marks. Would people be able to observe these in your school? What would they look for as evidence?

Organizational Assessment: Metaphoric Analysis

4. Now that you are familiar with using circle maps, it's time you considered a metaphor that best describes you as an instructional leader. In the center of your circle map, write your metaphor. In the circle around your metaphor, identify its core values.

5. Using a **multiflow map** (Hyerle, 1996), let's examine the causes and effects of a core value you have as an instructional leader. In the center rectangle, identify your core value (a value you would refuse to give an inch on even if your job were in jeopardy). On the left side, fill in the people, events, or experiences that helped create that value (in other words, where did that value come from?). On the right side of the map, focus on how this core value manifests in practice or the effects that result from acting on the core value. Add as many additional rectangles to the left or right as necessary. You do not need to have a one-to-one correlation between the causes and effects.

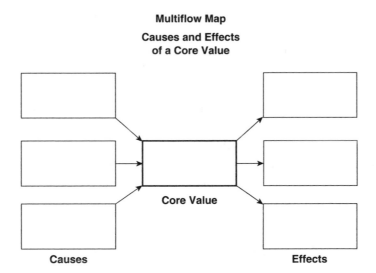

Multiflow Map

**Causes and Effects
of a Core Value**

Core Value

Causes   **Effects**

Metaphoric Reframing

A Vehicle for Creative Leadership

This chapter represents the "so what?" of the book's concept by discussing the significance of the three leadership archetypes in relation to contemporary research. A variety of noteworthy authors have acknowledged the importance of leaders' core values that address (1) a cause beyond oneself (Glickman, 2003), (2) creation and communication of shared vision (Argyris, 1964; Fullan, 2001; Gilligan, 1982; Wheatley, 1999), (3) people's need for finding meaning in their life and their work and in the role of school for providing that meaning (Bolman & Deal, 2003; Evans, 1996; Fullan, 2003; Sergiovanni, 1999), and (4) leadership behavior as outward manifestations of core commitments and personal mission (Beck & Murphy, 1993; Reeves, 2002; Spiegel, 1995). While appreciating inquiry about core values that inspire leaders, we believe the literature often accesses traditional and predictable pathways that only skim the surface of intrinsically deep and prevailing beliefs shaping administrative practice.

From our perspective, conventional methodologies have thus far failed to enter the intimate world of images reflecting personal and provocative beliefs that drive leaders' purpose and vision. Contemporary authors have developed noteworthy insights about leadership behavior that are theory based and reflect analysis of leaders' rationalizations for how and why they perform as they do. Through our lenses, however, we consider current efforts to have been unsuccessful in discovering the obvious—namely, that our logical-thought language provides a one-dimensional perspective. Our experience informs us that getting at the heart of leaders' moral purposes and innate dispositions requires an opening of new passages to insight and new modes of expression. We believe that those deep values that drive school leadership are accessible through the manifestation of imaginative and creative analogy. As we have seen in the previous chapters, one path through that threshold is storytelling, paved by metaphor.

A NEW LEADERSHIP FRAME

Since the summer of 2002, school leaders in all fifty states have participated in a professional development project funded by the Bill and Melinda Gates Foundation. Dan Cherry is the director of the project for New Hampshire. For the past three years, all New Hampshire participants completed a leadership orientation survey that included the four leadership frames developed by Bolman and Deal (structural, political, human resource, and symbolic) and two developed by Spiegel (spiritual and instructional). Analysis of the surveys revealed a strong identification with the spiritual frame characteristics by principals and superintendents. (See Resource for a description of the spiritual and instructional frames and their eight identifying characteristics.)

As principal-in-residence for the New Hampshire project, Jeff Spiegel has served in the capacity of field consultant to more than 200 principals and 100 superintendents. His interviews with school leaders focused on personal and professional purposes, values, and goals by way of metaphoric reframing. The dialogues provided a lens through which ideas took form and reflected individuals' encounters with their professional milieus and personal models of reality from another analytical context. Evidence from those interviews reinforced Beck and Murphy's (1993) contention that metaphors reside at a deep or root level of meaning and are a primary frame of reference for the ways in which school leaders view of the world. This was particularly true for one of our principals. By way of metaphor, she likened herself to the badger from *Wind in the Willows*, who built a home to improve his life and the lives of others. "It's his attention to detail," she observed. "It's the same feeling and intensity of making a connection to building a new home to feeling generous toward others and reminding ourselves that each one of us has a story to tell."

Comparative analysis of the metaphors with the results from the leadership orientation survey provided further evidence of the relationship between reflective thinking through metaphor and the value preferences of the spiritual leadership frame. Metaphors represented a variety of themes ranging from survival to maintenance to vision quest. As we read in previous chapter introductions of the three archetypes, reflections and references to their schools by leaders were characterized by artful prose and creative imagination.

Metaphors also reframed ideas to form other attributes beyond the meaning of their literal context. "My metaphor for who I am as a leader," reflected one principal, "is that I'm like a multifaceted diamond. I'm able to reflect the needs of others, and through the talents I've been endowed with as a moral person, I can lift their hopes and sing their praises."

REFRAMING OUR UNDERSTANDINGS ABOUT LEADERSHIP BY WAY OF OZ

Our process for considering compelling related works illustrates how the basic tenets in this book set us apart from the literature and provides a new vision about leadership behavior. Given that our work discusses the importance of metaphor as a tool for understanding, we thought we'd "walk our talk" by associating the protagonists in *The Wizard of Oz* to six contemporary authors who have led the discussion addressing leadership values and moral purposes.

From a developmental perspective, the work of the following authors inspired our effort to provide a different lens to describe another kind of leadership behavior. The moral "metanoic" (Greek for "fundamental shift of mind") or "outside the box" thinking that links leaders' core beliefs and intrinsic purposes with strategies they use to address complex and challenging problems today promotes and inspires spiritual leadership. "Tapping the power of your moral compass will be a way of guaranteeing that you are being true to yourself and the people you lead. Using this power means that you must *act*" (Brubaker & Coble, 2005, p. 182).

Douglas Reeves and David Sousa

Douglas Reeves and David Sousa both represent for us the Scarecrow's search for a brain or frame of mind. In *The Daily Disciplines of Leadership* (2002), Reeves acknowledges that "educational leaders must ultimately focus on their core values. Values should govern educational policy" (p. 33). He understands that personal mission is indicative of how leaders establish organizational priorities. "The strategic leader depends upon principles and values since they create context for every leadership decision within the system" (p. 91).

While we appreciate Reeves's effort to help leaders reflect on their leadership credos, his journey is restricted by a rational and analytic reflection process. As the Scarecrow, Reeves relies on traditional thinking. To reveal leaders' personal missions, he asks them to take a few minutes to identify their mission in writing and compare it with their organization's mission.

With the stories in our book, we've attempted to depict another way to access personal mission. Our leaders' metaphors and reframing through the various processes we'll discuss in Chapter 5 led to more provocative and insightful discoveries that revealed their intrinsic purposes and the foundations of their moral convictions. The "yellow brick road" we paved for them created a new avenue for alternative perspectives about our leaders' personal and professional missions and established an innovative route through imagery for identifying their core values. Here is how one principal reflected on her mission by way of metaphor:

> I see myself as *Everybody's Warm Fuzzy Blanket*. My office represents a safe and comforting place where kids, teachers, and parents can get their needs met. It comes from always wanting to be a teacher, someone who people can trust in order to grow.

Another principal reframed her work as a leader by considering this quote by William Irwin Thompson: "Like a lure-casting fisherman, man seems to cast a fantasy far in front of him and then slowly reels himself into it." Subsequently, she observed, "I liked those words because, in hindsight, I've discovered incredible power in imagining possibilities that led to surprising achievements."

Like the Scarecrow's search, David Sousa's work represents a search for mind by developing a compelling argument for creative leadership thinking in his book *The Leadership Brain* (2003). According to Sousa, creative leaders are different from managers because they find ways to discover imaginative, nontraditional solutions to problems within their organizations. These types of leaders are endowed with a broad knowledge of educational theory, an ability to analyze complex and situational problems, and a predilection for conceptualizing ways to bring about change.

Sousa believes that leaders who seek to develop creative organizations can only do so by encouraging others to question standard practices, particularly if they are not working; to create a prevailing culture that welcomes constructive criticism and innovative thinking; and to find ways to link creative thinking with discussions about schools' missions.

The vehicle for accessing creative thinking, according to Sousa, is by way of imagery or visualization. Imagery takes the form of *imaging,* the visualization of past experience, or *imagining,* the depiction of something not experienced. Sousa provides examples and proposes activities that use visualization as a way to arrive at creative thinking.

We are indebted to Sousa's valuable contribution to creative leadership thinking. However, his suggested approaches are limited to visualization and therefore provide few avenues for using right-brain thinking for problem solving, decision making, and the revelation of intrinsic values that motivate leadership behavior. In the subsequent chapter, we'll describe both a process for accessing the creative, nonrational mind and approaches using nontraditional thinking to activate right-brain strategies for outside-the-box problem solving and creation of organizational thinking in more imaginative and fulfilling ways. We call these metaphoric reframing techniques *sensings,* or the development of extemporaneously derived images, thoughts, and feelings that take the form of symbols or metaphors that describe past experiences or, as our principal, David, demonstrated, imagined possibilities.

When *sensings* are created, primary-process thinking occurs. This type of thinking relies on our intuitive understandings of experiences from both our real and imaginative worlds. The portrayal of thinking that emerges from primary process as a symbol or metaphor somehow makes sense to us in ways previously not discovered. *Sensings* can be expressed by way of metaphoric reframing and in a variety of genres ranging from spontaneous art renderings to unrehearsed poetry and prose and impromptu music, movement, or dance.

One principal enjoyed painting as a personal form of expression and a way to relieve stress in his life. Over time, he began experimenting with drawing as a way to tackle the problems he was addressing as a leader. We consider this principal's process for using artwork as representative of the side of mind Sousa believed creative leaders use.

> Often as I drew, the problem I was grappling with would reappear in my mind. Whenever I reflected on my artwork afterward, I discovered certain patterns . . . which somehow suggested ideas related to the complex issues I was attempting to resolve. It was as if I had discovered a new way to access another perspective.

Sousa also makes a significant contribution to the literature by acknowledging the importance of spiritual thinking in our schools. He discusses how this type of thinking moves beyond the rational discourse and analytic approaches that we witness in our classrooms and faculty meetings. Sousa proposes a mindfulness that involves searching within oneself to interpret and understand the world. He believes that school leaders are driven by forces of spirituality in which public and private work are aligned with personal values.

While we wholeheartedly agree with Sousa's conclusions, we were struck by his omission in not describing ways for leaders to identify their intrinsic purposes and core beliefs by way of primary-process thinking. In contrast to his belief that leaders need to become adept at being creative and accessing intuitive imaging for identifying issues, problems, and solutions, his questions for readers that are borrowed from Kaiser (2002) are designed for analytic and rational reflection. Sousa understands that we need to develop new and provocative road maps to access creative thought and to get closer to linking intrinsic values with our work. But he fails to identify the appropriate vehicles for gaining such access. We hope to address that dilemma in subsequent discussions addressing *sensing* evaluations, metaphoric reframing, and primary-process thinking.

Robert Evans

Contrast Reeves as the Scarecrow with author Robert Evans. Evans's focus on leaders' values reminds us of the Tin Man in search of a heart. Evans calls for a new kind of leadership that "emphasizes authenticity, translating integrity, core beliefs and natural strengths of school leaders into practical strategies for problem-solving" (1996, p. xiii). We agree that leadership begins at one's center: "Authentic leaders build their practice outward from the core commitments rather than inward from a management text" (p. 193). But where might we find Evans's road map to revealing those core commitments?

Evans conveys a theory for creating vision that acknowledges the need for different structures of analysis. "Largely overlooked in all the enthusiasm for vision is that it typically derives from a personal and imaginative creativity that [transcends] . . . analysis" (1996, p. 210). While we embrace his perspective about the importance of understanding the mental models of leaders (what Sergiovanni refers to as "mind frames"), we nevertheless propose a more engaging pathway for understanding leadership behavior.

As previous chapters illustrated, thematic archetypes act as cognitive and spiritual guides for deconstructing images and analogies that describe reality from another dimension of mind. Archetypes represent "innate dispositions for specific kinds of thought and behavior" (Feinstein & Krippner, 1988). Our book incorporates thematic analysis of personal stories to bridge the gap between the head and the heart, the left and the right brain. Our purpose aims at producing a more holistic and integrated presentation

of ideas, beliefs, commitments, and values that explain leadership dispositions and organizational behavior by way of metaphor. Consider the words
of the principal who reframed himself as the *Nuts and Bolts Guy*:

> "I like to fix things and get my hands dirty," he says with a smile.
> "My father was a self-taught immigrant and a natural teacher. He
> taught me to be curious and gave me the skills to listen to people,
> to give back to the community. That's helped me try to understand
> people, get everyone here at school on the same page. It's also why
> as Kiwanis Director of the Key Club International program I'm
> proud in having taken 200 kids to Boston to teach them
> leadership skills."

Michael Fullan

Michael Fullan's discussion of what is at the core of leaders' moral
purpose also reminds us of the Tin Man's search for heart. He contends
that acting with the intention of making a positive difference in the lives
of people and society as a whole is a core commitment and requirement
for contemporary leaders (2001, p. 3). In Fullan's work, there is compelling evidence that principals are able to describe their moral purposes,
communicate them to their faculties, and seek to integrate them into
the organization's mission. His stories about leaders reflect the generative
archetypes of an ethic of care, a cause beyond oneself, and a search for
contributing in a positive way to society as a whole.

But where did the leaders' beliefs come from? Fullan doesn't provide
any evidence informing us how such deep and enduring values became
ingrained in leaders' sense of moral purpose and vision or how they
became instructive guides for their work.

The stories in the previous chapters attempt to dig deeper into the psy-
che of school leaders by addressing the following questions: Were their
intrinsic purposes acquired from family upbringing? Were they realized
from significant events in the leaders' personal or professional lives? Or
were they incorporated from religious, spiritual, or political involvement?
Discovering the roots to such firmly held moral convictions is instructive
for developing cultural change in any organization. Current authors leave
us to simply imagine what those influences were and how they shaped the
credos of moral leadership. Here's how a high school principal reframed
his sense of self and described the roots of his metaphor:

> The Giving Tree is a metaphor of my leadership style. The sense of
> "giver" is best exemplified by the stories of four powerful women

I have admired for their efforts and sacrifices. Within each, I viewed an aspect of myself that I would like to cultivate. Each gave without a conscious thought because it was a reflection of the people they were. Their stories, like countless other "givers," are stories I hope I may someday honor by imitation. I would also like to be thought of as a "giver."

Lee Bolman and Terrence Deal

Bolman and Deal represent for us the Lion in search of courage. We consider their book *Leading With Soul: An Uncommon Journey of Spirit* (2001) a courageous exploration into the spiritual underpinnings of leadership. Like Fullan, they've investigated moral purpose and acknowledged that culture and core values are increasingly vital as the social glue fusing organizations with both passion and principle (p. 178).

Bolman and Deal (2003) also developed a leadership orientation instrument with four conceptual frames: human resource, political, symbolic, and structural. Each frame contained eight characteristics describing leadership behavior. Interestingly, when we added a fifth frame, spiritual, and administered it to more than 150 school administrators during the last two years, we were surprised to discover that the latter frame received the second highest rating. The significance of this finding suggests that leaders often view their work as reflecting a need to fulfill intrinsic purposes and to acknowledge their role as encouraging personal transformation for self and others. Furthermore, comparative analysis between leaders' metaphors and leadership orientation results established the efficacy of this new frame of analysis and the strong connection between its eight identifying principles and leaders' personal sense of mission and core commitments.

Our response to Fullan's and Bolman's and Deal's work is to provide a guide or approach in the form of what we call "sensing" experiences. This technique liberates people from their rational understandings of self and moral purpose to reveal core beliefs linking personal and professional mission. Our road map borrows from Dorothy's vision quest for inner truth, wisdom, and intrinsic purpose. Our process provides an alternative pathway or "yellow brick road of a second kind" that leads to the creation of visual or tangible images derived by way of storytelling and metaphor.

These *sensings* are accessed by way of primary-process thinking. Sometimes they stimulate the creation of abstract symbols or repeatable elements that describe leaders' feelings and perceptual experiences. Often, the *sensings* represented some larger meaning or set of meanings about leaders' lives and interactions.

The *sensings* derived from primary-process thinking represented the formation of metaphoric images that tapped into leaders' intuitive understandings of experience from both their real and imaginative worlds. They portrayed thinking that emerged as abstract and sometimes disconnected symbols or metaphors that made sense to the leaders in some intangible and inexplicable ways. Simply stated, they felt right. During primary-process thinking, the leaders' ideas, thoughts, and concepts existed harmoniously and simultaneously. What materialized were archetypal themes that often led to some epiphany or inner truth. One principal reframed herself as the *Gypsy* and described why her pseudonym was an apt metaphor of unconditional love for her personal and professional "selves."

> My concept of the gypsy has that kind of perspective to travel, to go to other places, to be open to people. Maybe the gypsy metaphor is the vehicle or the mechanism or the process, and the unconditional love is the goal or the content.

Our book provides other examples of how sensing conversations led to the development of metaphoric images leaders created to describe their work contexts, their core values, and the connection of personal and professional missions. We describe how leaders accessed intuitive instincts to reveal their intrinsic purposes much in the manner of Dorothy's outward journey and inward search for meaning. Dorothy took the risk of selecting a novel and evocative path to self-discovery, and the imaginative leaders we describe arrived at self-revelation.

> We are truly entering a twilight period, and like the old *Twilight Zone* series of the mid-twentieth century, we are "traveling through another dimension: a dimension not only of sight and sound but of mind; a journey into a wondrous land whose boundaries are that of imagination." That is the danger and the opportunity for educational leaders. (Houston, 2003)

The underlying purpose of this chapter is to acknowledge the influence of metaphoric reframing on our understanding of school leadership behavior as well as personal development. For that reason, we include a brief story about how David learned to think metaphorically in terms of personal life issues and subsequently about his role as a leader. His discovery of another voice and an alternative perspective through which to see himself, his professional colleagues, and his institution's behavior reveals meaningful insights for the reader to consider.

If spirituality, as Joseph Campbell suggested, is the discovery of that inward thing we basically are, then David's use of metaphor represents a powerful illustration of how his reframing led to epiphany and the recognition of guiding personal myths. As we have seen, the evolution of David was characterized by a compelling story of transformation and a vivid description of one leader's spiritual journey.

PERSONAL MYTHS: SPIRITUAL GUIDES FOR LEADERS

David's personal myth during his early years revolved around the victim. Through his experiences with therapy, experimentation with imagery, and utilization of reframing in the workplace, David's personal myth evolved toward the more positive image of hero. When we consider the representatives of the other archetypes in this book, we meet similar images representing the personal myths that guide leaders. The Ambassador, who also fell prey to personal health issues, was driven by a desire to create positive change. Everybody's Parent was motivated by an ethic of care.

Personal myths characterized the root metaphor or frame that described and enhanced understanding of leadership and organizational behaviors by the principals described in this book. By considering their personal and professional histories, their values and beliefs, their favorite stories and most admired heroines and heroes, a constellation of metaphors emerged around separate yet connected core themes. In a sense, all of the principals in this book held commonly shared myths about their purposes that were characterized by a personal ethic of care and a devotion to a cause beyond oneself.

These personal myths constitute a theoretical and organizational concept aimed at distinguishing administrators' professional goals and behaviors in light of guiding visions and prevailing purposes. Personal myths represent a new paradigm for reframing the context of administrative behavior and for creating a novel approach for understanding the unique and diverse journeys of people who lead.

For some of our leaders, personal myths often appeared as images of knowing that remained dormant until, through some awakening, they demonstrated an understanding of themselves, their past, and their organizational culture that transcended their rational comprehension and explanation. By looking back, inward, and forward metaphorically, these leaders found personal myths that provided provocative insights into the ways in which they structured their lives and the methods by which their institutions reflected their intrinsic beliefs on a broader scale.

Consider the stories of each of the principals in this book. The use of metaphor represented a context for understanding administrative practice as a reaching out, a way of trying new structures of life in schools. The personal myths that emerged from the metaphoric reframing process represented self-instructive stories as well as narratives about their relationships with the outside world. Their myths were both progressive and regressive. They provided opportunities for school leaders to identify contradictions while revealing new insights and goals.

When the metaphors leading to personal myths are accessed, new perspectives about the relationship between and among people and their contexts change. Having school administrators reflect on their myths and apply them to their decisions leads to the potential for new discoveries and the questioning of former, self-limiting beliefs. Personal myth analysis also poses interesting implications for accessing the whole mind and connecting thought processes to a potentially more holistic understanding of self, others, and institutions.

REFLECTION QUESTIONS AND ACTIVITIES

Leadership Assessment: Spiritual Frame Analysis

Here are some characteristics of a **spiritual** leader:

- I identify my work with some intrinsic purpose or goal.
- I consider my role as linked to some personal value or goal.
- I consider the school and its functions as part of a larger whole.
- I strive to have people connect personal and professional goals.
- I encourage people to realize their full potential.
- I view change as a necessary and never-ending process.
- I view problems and failures as benchmarks for change.
- I consider the school a place for personal transformation.

Put a "+" symbol next to each characteristic that describes your everyday practice. It should be a trait that you have so well established that you could demonstrate its effectiveness to other leaders. Put an *N* next to each characteristic that you feel you need more work on in the way of professional development, coursework, or dialogue.

Reflect on being a spiritual leader. How do you pull the pendulum back to create balance between the management of a school and the spiritual leadership of a school?

Look back at the eight characteristics. Look at the "+" marks. Would people be able to observe these in your school? What would you look for as evidence?

Organizational Assessment: Metaphoric Analysis

Think of a favorite fictional character or person you admire. Who is it? Describe the character's or person's most appealing qualities. Now describe any objectionable traits. Make the same lists for your qualities. (We intentionally chose our fictional character to demonstrate that you can push the limits of this exercise and still gain quality insights about your leadership style.)

Now compare and contrast the appealing and objectionable traits of your fictional or real person with your own. What did you discover?

Here are three questions a fictional character such as Bugs Bunny might ask you about school leadership:

1. What's up, Doc?

2. So, Doc, when should you have taken a left turn at Albuquerque?

3. Eh, Doc, when's the last time you said, "I'll do it, but I'll probably hate myself in the morning"?

Here are three questions an admired person such as Dr. Martin Luther King Jr. might ask about school leadership:

1. How do you ensure equitable opportunities for minority students?

2. I had a dream about leadership. What's yours?

3. As a school leader, what are you willing to fight for?

Consider three questions your fictional character or admirable person might ask you about school leadership. What might those questions be? Write them down and answer them. What did you discover?

Road Maps to Organizational Success

This chapter begins with a brief history tracing the use of metaphor as a vehicle for understanding leaders and organizations. This background will help readers appreciate how prior research led to the creation of this book and its focus on the ways metaphoric reframing can enhance institutional development in business and education. We'll then transition to the "now what?" of the book and offer specific strategies for moving people and organizations from familiar places, where prevailing and perhaps negative practices are entrenched, to more enlightened, inspired, and refocused initiatives.

As discussed in Chapter 4, some of the strategies we describe are called *sensings* because they access a variety of cognitive and creative modalities for metaphoric thinking. Sensings take form in response to prompts such as personal artifacts, favorite fairy tales, storybook themes, inanimate objects, or icons.

THE ROLE OF METAPHOR FOR ORGANIZATIONAL AND LEADERSHIP DEVELOPMENT

The use of metaphors to understand organizations and leadership behavior is not new. Morgan (1986) assessed various types of organizational structures and processes that drive institutions. By exploring metaphoric images that defined people's interactions and behaviors, Morgan was able to identify a process for diagnosing institutional problems and create new ways to understand organizations. His focus on key metaphors gave special meaning to the influence they exert in analyzing behavior. Metaphors formed a context that produced special insights about generally complex and often paradoxical trends within institutions. This finding was particularly relevant to David's context in Chapter 2 when he unveiled the victim mythology to his faculty. It was a prime example of a leader diagnosing a pattern of institutional problems by way of analogy and prescribing a behavioral shift with a new metaphor.

Beck and Murphy (1993) developed a strategy for constructing meaning about educational leaders by examining the language principals use when they discuss their work. The authors moved beyond self-conscious structural analysis to access the essence of the principalship in more evocative ways. From their analysis, they discovered very unique insights by leaders that confirmed earlier findings by Owens and Steinhoff (1988) in their study of organizations.

For these writers, metaphors helped clarify the meaning of abstract concepts; the writers compared analogies to more concrete and understandable ideas. Metaphors helped elicit pictures, likening an individual or object of analysis to both cognitive and affective domains. In a similar regard, the use of metaphoric reframing during the interviews with principals we've discussed in previous chapters dramatized the way leaders were able to examine their core values and intrinsic beliefs and connect those influences to their administrative behaviors.

Kreffing and Frost's (1984) multimetaphor perspective on managing organizational culture helped identify unconscious forces that were often difficult to predict or tightly control. The authors believed metaphors provided greater capacities for exposing the complexities and contradictions characterizing organizational culture. They concluded that metaphors were effective for framing desired changes that could lead to the development of a new culture.

Kolbenschlag (1988) contended that metaphors not only reflect behavior and personal values but also possess the power to create social change. This is particularly relevant to the way David, in Chapter 3, reframed the faculty's traditional thinking about recess to create the metaphor of recreation education. In Chapter 4, David helped the adults as well as the children reframe the loss of the trees by identifying a grieving metaphor that redefined their context, assisted individual and group healing, and linked those phenomena to best instructional practices.

Organizational metaphors function in various ways. They chunk information succinctly and provide coherent wholes to defining a set of behaviors, a group, or an institution (Lakoff & Johnson, 1980; Ortony, 1975). As we've seen from the essays by the principals, metaphors can be original and vivid and can require an effort of reflection that plays an important role in the process of individuation whereby people in later life recognize archetypes as part of their developmental process (Jung, 1953).

Let's consider some ways to use metaphoric thinking in the organizational context. Many of these strategies can help individuals identify former self-limiting beliefs, assist group problem solving, create organizational vision, ensure institutional commitment, and encourage acceptance for change.

USING METAPHORS TO IDENTIFY CORE VALUES AND INTRINSIC BELIEFS

Writing Prompts

Following many of the interviews with principals, we developed a framework that helped guide leaders' descriptions and deeper analysis of their metaphors. The framework was characterized by a series of reflection questions to stimulate deeper insights about their metaphor. Leaders were asked to consider how their metaphor evolved during the unfolding of their personal history (essentially, the metaphor's historical roots), what core values characterized the metaphor, where in their professional work the metaphor was relevant, and how the metaphor instructed their intrinsic beliefs. The authors of "The U.S. Ambassador of Change," "I Am the Father of 1,453 children Plus 2, With a Large Extended Family," and "The Evolution of a Leadership Metaphor" wrote in response to the following prompt. We invite you to participate in the same activity and to consider using this framework with individuals within your organization to more clearly understand what values and beliefs motivate their work ethic and behaviors.

Questions and Reflections to Consider

Tell the Story of Your Metaphor

Reflect on the metaphor that best describes you as a leader. Try to describe it as fully as possible.

A. You might wish to think about an artifact that exemplifies your metaphor. If so, try to weave it into your essay.

B. You can also develop poems, songs, paintings, or any other kind of creative medium to enhance your description.

Critical to your essay is an explanation of the values that underscore your metaphor. What values are at the core of your metaphor, and more important, where did they come from (e.g., upbringing, critical events in your life, influences from others, deep beliefs or feelings)?

Try to explain how your metaphor relates to your work context, particularly how it is relevant to you as a school leader. Provide some specific examples. *Can you cite an instance or a significant experience that best demonstrates how your metaphor manifested itself?*

Also consider how your metaphor has worked for and/or against you. *What did your metaphor teach you? What did you learn from such experiences?*

Thematic Analysis of a Favorite Storybook or Fairy Tale

The Badger, the Gypsy, and Everybody's Mother

Another way we simulated leaders' creative thinking was by way of thematic analysis of their favorite fairy tale or storybook. Some principals were able immediately to discuss the central themes of their fairy tale and attach significance of the story to their work and personal values. When leaders spoke metaphorically about their work and school settings, their reflections represented both a deconstruction of storybook themes and a reconstruction of professional purpose.

One principal likened herself to the badger in Kenneth Grahame's *Wind in the Willows* (1989). She described the story as depicting the compelling adventures of forest creatures living in a community marked by harmonious but sometimes antagonistic relationships. She thought its appeal was in the vivid, intensely rich world of images. For this principal, the story's central theme was the longing for home: "It's coming to some understanding as to what constitutes home. It's Mole catching a whiff, Toad always back at Toad Hall, Ratty, dear Ratty, loving the riverbank."

When asked to describe the resolution of the story's central issue, this leader responded, "It's not entirely resolved. You just get to a new plateau of understanding." She then identified an alternate theme: "Life is in the journey."

This principal explained how the world is filled with remarkable strangers and that life as a journey is an ongoing revelation of the mysteries of the Earth, whether of plants, animals, or people. She was adept at connecting the story's theme to her work with beginning teachers. Her sense of creating a nurturing environment for novices was revealed in a paragraph from an article she wrote. It related well to the core values of the Parent archetype.

Much of the labor is in the nest building, building a home. Feeling at home meant feeling safe to explore, to strike out in unexpected directions, to establish a personal identity. Feeling at home as a school professional means both that one is welcomed as an individual within the professional community and that one takes responsibility for seeking and establishing a personal identity. It's a real determination to look at the quality of life for self and others.

Another principal identified *A Wrinkle in Time* (1962) by Madeleine L'Engle as her favorite storybook. This narrative represented an intriguing fantasy about the disappearance of a father and son into a time dimension (a wrinkle in time). The protagonists are captured by evil witches. Meg, the daughter and sibling, struggles to find them and ultimately becomes their liberator.

This leader identified two primary themes in the book: the triumph of good over evil and getting in touch with feelings. She discussed the importance of valuing feelings in a cold, technological environment. Most of all, she was delighted to talk about the book and what it meant to her in terms of connectedness.

> I loved the story. I loved the group of students I shared it with. The students and I experienced it together. [It was] . . . a real bonding. I've given copies to my sister. I've read the book to my children and given them copies. A lot of it is in the sharing of it. It's emotionally powerful.

As she continued to reflect on the fairy tale, this leader noticed the unifying link between the themes of good over evil and valuing feelings residing in the power of love.

> I really believe in the power of love and unlocking of the gates of control. The story's fundamental message is that the absolute power of love is the acting on it and communication of it. Unconditional love . . . it creates a connection, a bond.

Like the previous principal, the Badger, this leader was quick to relate the book's themes to her work, her notion of who she was as a global citizen, and her vision of social consciousness. She concluded that an apt metaphor for herself was the Gypsy because it represented her desire to travel to different countries in an attempt to understand people and to appreciate the cultural diversity of our world. Again, the Parent archetype seems an appropriate characterization for the ethic of care that underscores the Gypsy's core values and intrinsic beliefs.

I believe in a global spiritual connection, with love as the unifying element. I suspect that without that belief, I couldn't do this job. Also, through that connectedness [love] I believe it can unite people and provide the supports that connect people on our jobs. That's our job as a people; we become unified. I hope my students become aware of their connections to other kids and that we all have responsibility for one another.

A third principal marveled over *The Little Prince* by Antoine de Saint-Exupéry (1943). This is a poignant tale about a small prince who lives alone on a tiny planet. Through his encounters with characters on his planet and on Earth, the little prince discovers what's important in life.

This leader loved the story for its charm and unabashed sentimentality. Like the previous principals, the fairy tale elicited strong emotions for this leader. "It makes me cry every time. It taps into the same thing *E.T.* taps into. It's pretty primitive. It taps into very early needs to be loved, to have someone special."

As she continued to analyze the story, this principal viewed *The Little Prince* as a central showcase for the socialized adult and for the child. According to her, the story provides clear statements about the meaning of relationships and life. She likened herself to Everybody's Mother and acknowledged her parental perspective in connecting with teachers and students.

One of the truths is that, when you love somebody, what's special about that person is that that person loves you. It's the relationship that makes it special. The rose looks like every other, but his [the little prince's] rose is special. It belongs to him, and when he looks out on the universe he knows his special rose is out there somewhere.

This leader admired the gentle sense of irony in the dedication of the book. It's with an apology to all children for dedicating it to his friend, an adult. The principal liked how the author rededicated the book to his friend when he was a little boy.

For this principal, the central problem of the story was the little prince's search for answers about the meaning of life. Through his encounters with each character, the little prince uncovers much about the mysteries of life. This leader reflected on the book's themes and close connection to her work, particularly as it addressed the concept of being special.

"Unique au monde." It means unique in the world. The little prince sees his rose as unique. He cries because he discovers others that look like her. He then has to learn what it is that makes her special. . . . At school we work hard to make every single child feel special and loved and deserving of good treatment.

Reflecting on her experiences as a school administrator, this leader identified with the pilot in *The Little Prince.* She likened his predicament to her own at school. The image of the aviator's circumstances compelled her to recognize a deeper understanding of who she was as a principal.

He's stuck in the middle out in the desert, and his plane won't run. . . . I very frequently feel I'm alone as a principal. As close as I am with the staff, I continually get surprised that they still see me as the principal. It's either to my fault or to my credit. . . . Ultimately, it's me as principal. Even though I'm surrounded by people who like me, I feel alone.

With elements of the Touchstone archetype, this leader acknowledged a close connection to the pilot's personal growth and her sense of self as an anchor and trusted professional by her colleagues.

He learns so much from the little prince, but he learns he has so much wisdom himself to share. You can liken [this school] to the desert. I feel I can learn from everyone here, like the aviator and the little prince, and yet, like them, I have much wisdom to share and . . . people look to me for that.

Struck by the similarities of the pilot's plight in the story and her own challenges starting out in her current school, this leader discussed the aviator's openness and saw a connection to her own beliefs.

I liked how he handled being stuck in the desert. He didn't lose it. He took it as it came. He didn't panic, didn't cry, "Why me?" He was cool with handling a fairly real-life terrifying situation. . . . [He] casually accepts his situation. I've handled the situation, which is analogous to crashing in the desert, with a certain amount of terror. . . . I saw our school back then as a desert metaphor. . . . Like a desert, the school had hidden secrets. . . . It was a matter of discovering the secrets and pulling out a few bad roots.

These examples of metaphoric reframing by way of storybook themes and central characters represent one avenue in which leaders are able to reflect on their work and associate their mission with core values. The metaphors generated by the principals were thoughtfully arrived at and imaginatively reflected their sense of self over time.

The Badger, while adopting the character from her fairy tale, nevertheless applied a process of reflecting back and forth between the story protagonist and herself to develop personal theories and analyses of her evolution and current work behavior. The Badger metaphor also withstood its relevance when compared to characterizations of her by faculty members.

The Gypsy represented a projection of that leader's view of herself as a globally conscious citizen. Her value orientation to her role as principal and her personal desire to travel and immerse herself in different cultures symbolized for her a gypsy wandering from land to land: "a gypsy is what I really am."

Everybody's Mother viewed her metaphor as reflecting her natural tendencies to "direct and fix and manage everything." Her sense of self as a fixer and a director and a manager was "a fairly common female thing." The importance of this leader's recognition of her professional mission also manifested the discovery of her voice as both a woman and a leader.

USING METAPHORS TO ASSESS FACULTY PERCEPTIONS ABOUT THEIR LEADER AND THEIR SCHOOL

Metaphors are an extremely effective and nonthreatening tool for gaining insights about the quality of leadership and school organization perceived by school members. Consider some of the metaphors developed by professionals at the Badger's, the Gypsy's, and Everybody's Mother's schools.

The Badger

School Metaphor	Ideal Leader Metaphor	Principal Metaphor
Dry-Docked Ship	Director	Shipyard Foreman
Family Under Stress	Lead by Modeling	Overworked Boss

The Gypsy

School Metaphor	Ideal Leader Metaphor	Principal Metaphor
Skating Rink	Community Person	Mother Teresa
Extended Family	People/Process Oriented	Mensch

Everybody's Mother

School Metaphor	Ideal Leader Metaphor	Principal Metaphor
Bubbling Iron Pot	Nourisher	Primary Stirrer
Circus	Ringmaster	Ringmaster

While the context for these metaphors focused on the principals, they nevertheless paralleled themes that characterized colleagues' metaphors for their schools. The Badger had so many brushfires, she was perceived as rushing from job to job to patch up each crisis. As a foreman, she was considered overworked and difficult to access. Yet she was acknowledged for her efforts to bring out the best in her teachers—noteworthy because the staff was often under stress.

Metaphors for the Gypsy were extremely positive, viewing her as accepting challenges in a positive fashion, practicing shared decision making and working tirelessly to meet everyone's needs, a real "mensch" (a Yiddish word for a good, caring person).

Everybody's Mother was perceived as a leader in total command of her school. All of the colleague metaphors painted her as a focused leader using her acumen to judge when and how to move the school and staff to increased effectiveness. The metaphoric reflection process motivated one colleague to use poetic imagery to describe the school's troubled past and the principal's positive influence: "She guides us through the winds of change and the currents of conflict to reach our destination. The teachers being the sails, not resisting the wind but embracing it."

The colleague metaphors for these schools and their leaders represented a creative reframing process that presented their institutions as complex cultures powered by leaders who possessed strong ideals and devotion to noteworthy goals. While each school was unique and characterized by local influences, the metaphors of colleagues exposed insightful perspectives about the realities of their schools.

Developmentally, two schools (the Gypsy's and Everybody's Mother's) were moving progressively toward the visions that reflected the core values and intrinsic beliefs of their principals. This is not an uncommon phenomenon. Often, schools take on the expressed as well as the subconsciously conveyed values and beliefs of their leader.

The Badger's school, regarded in the past as a fine public institution, appeared from the metaphors to be mired in conflict with a leader who, although highly regarded by colleagues, was unable to propel the school forward to accomplish the goals and aspirations that characterized her beliefs. As one colleague so poignantly put it:

[She] . . . doesn't really lead in the sense that she gathers everyone around and inspires with the visions of where the group could go with a commonly held goal. This dancer is a part of the group and yet set apart.

We continue to be amazed at the power metaphoric reframing possesses for illuminating the attitudes, perceptions, and feelings held by members in educational institutions. Recently, one of the authors was invited to a school district to help administrators gain a clearer understanding of their school cultures with the goal of ensuring that everyone within the schools was working toward a common vision. When asked to describe in metaphor what it was like working in their schools, here's what elementary school teachers said:

Elementary School Metaphors

Working at the elementary school is like . . .

1. a roller coaster—ups/downs. You end where you started.

2. ☯

3. working at the monkey house in the zoo.

4. watching the sand shift in an hour glass—we see the kids going downhill no matter how hard we work.

5. being on duty in the military in the streets of Baghdad.

6. walking a tightrope.

7. the social networking of animals (primates). Some days you are in good favor, some days bad favor, all depending on some trivial detail (animals)—if you hunted that day, puffed your feathers, etc.

8. cheese—individually wrapped.

9. a real adventure.

10. pushing a cart with square wheels. Progress is slow.

11. a yo-yo.

12. a day at the beach with a few rough waves.

13. watching a weather report, always unpredictable.

14. a community of many different minds! Everyone going in separate directions with some people following each other.

15. running a relay race and knowing everyone is running in the right direction without the baton.

16. an oasis in a desert. We arc so lucky here (most of the time).

17. walking on eggshells—it is safer to keep to yourself than risk saying or doing something viewed as wrong.

18. cutting a steak with a butter knife. Great intentions but less than stellar tools.

19. watching a home movie.

20. the Mid-Atlantic Ridge. The older teachers and newer teachers move further apart ("not everyone, though").

These were some pretty powerful images for what appears to be a school in crisis.

What do the images tell us? Clearly, strong, focused leadership does not appear to be evident in those metaphors describing student behavior, decision making, collaboration, or the community of teachers. Consider the images: a roller coaster, a monkey house, the streets of Baghdad, a tightrope, unpredictable weather, a yo-yo, the Mid-Atlantic Ridge with old and new teachers moving further apart.

If that's the school, what's the leader like? Some days you're in good favor, some days you're not, depending on some trivial detail, everyone running in the right direction without the baton, walking on eggshells, and everyone going in separate directions with some following each other.

What a powerful assessment of a school culture! The ability of metaphor to expose emotional and analytic perspectives provides a useful tool for addressing institutional reform efforts. Metaphors used by colleagues help create frames that allow an idea to form other characteristics or attributes beyond the meaning of their literal context. As disturbing as the elementary school metaphors are, they create the potential for generating new meanings and ideas. By encouraging teachers to communicate their personal realities, their metaphors lent support for reorganizing and reforming their cultural domain.

If we look more closely at the metaphors we can discern a sense of responsibility teachers have to their students, to each other, and to the school community. What are they saying? They want a commonly shared vision for their school. They want a leader who will command respect, maintain student discipline, deliver clear direction, provide appropriate resources, and build trust. They want a collegial atmosphere where new and veteran teachers can work collaboratively. Most of all, they want to be acknowledged for their accomplishments and have recognized those areas where progress has been made.

Now let's consider the metaphors from the high school.

High School Metaphors

Working at the high school is like . . .

1. working on a puzzle and not knowing where some pieces go—or if you even have them all!

2. going to a buffet—everyone is different.

3. a great car that just needs a little tune-up.

4. being stranded on a desert island with little water.

5. playing hide-and-seek.

6. ice-skating up a hill—difficult but not impossible.

7. a good picnic, without the booze.

8. building a bridge; always trying to connect the gaps.

9. putting a square peg in a round hole.

10. pushing a boulder—slowly inching forward.

11. a high school clique.

12. being with birds who put their heads in the sand.

13. a stairwell.

14. being on a roller coaster—it has its ups and downs.

15. is rarely dull.

16. being the only human on an alien planet (the kids are the aliens).

17. entertaining.

18. a box of chocolates—you never know what you are going to get.

Here again, we have a variety of images that suggest confusion about equitable distribution of resources, diversity without cohesion, challenging expectations, lack of receptivity to collaboration and new ideas, and estrangement from students.

What do these metaphors suggest about the leader? Teachers are feeling unappreciated for their efforts. The leader has not been successful in establishing a collaborative community of workers. Cliques suggest favoritism and disunity. There is a sense that the school is out of balance or has failed to find some equilibrium between how students and teachers embrace the school. The leader has not created a climate that encourages openness to change, new ideas, or proactive approaches to problem solving. The leader is not aware of the isolation felt by some teachers and the undercurrent of cynicism that characterizes "parking lot" discussions by staff.

Like those of their elementary school counterparts, the high school teachers' metaphors also suggested a desire for cooperation and collaboration. They want consistency and clear expectations. They want to know where they should be headed, provided with appropriate resources to get them there, and acknowledgment for working in a challenging environment.

For both the elementary and the high school faculties, metaphoric reframing helped identify core themes that explained colleagues' attitudes about their school and leader as well as their own behaviors in the workplace. By exposing the underlying values inherent in each teacher's metaphor and by analyzing those images globally, we were able to get glimpses of each educator's intrinsic purpose as a professional.

USING ARTIFACTS AS METAPHORS FOR DESCRIBING PROFESSIONAL MISSION AND PURPOSE

Have you ever noticed how principals decorate their offices? A broad range of artifacts characterizes what leaders display in their workspaces. Typical in most offices are the photos of family on window ledges with framed diplomas on the walls. But others can be more ornate and expansive. One leader was a volunteer fireman and a collector of firefighter paraphernalia. His office looked more like a museum, with neatly arranged shelves of fire truck reproductions, paintings of firemen, and even a life-sized fire hydrant! When asked how these artifacts reflected his work as a principal, this leader talked about saving lives and ensuring safety much like what he hoped his school did when preparing students for the real world and the unforeseen events in their lives.

Artifacts are meaningful tools for accessing metaphoric thinking about people's professional purposes and intrinsic beliefs. Artifact reflection involves convergent thinking that processes information around a common image so that thoughts and ideas can emerge from different directions into a unified and holistic view. From our discussions with principals, we discovered how artifacts provide an intriguing context through which leaders were able to reflect on their roles and behaviors.

A middle school principal's artifacts were related to nature. There were photographs of her yellow garden, with neat rows of tulip, iris, potentilla, rudbeckia, and blacked-eyed susan. She described her love of the outdoors and acknowledged the connection of nature to being a detail-oriented leader.

> When I'm gardening, there's something elemental about it, the soil and roots and digging in the earth. I love camping in a tent by a nearby pond. I like the details that are right there.

Her vision of nature was entwined with her sense of leadership style and purpose. She felt inclined to "hold the line" and "take refuge" in what was familiar, safe, and comforting.

Another principal kept her special artifacts in a large bucket in the corner of her office. In it were postcards from England, photographs of Latin America, and a backpack for skiing, hiking, journaling, plus a passport and a mountain bike book. She kept them there as reminders about travel to many places around the world and her work with children. She linked her interest in travel to the way she approached her work as a principal. Her artifacts represented her trust in the natural flow of events and the challenges she often faced being in different parts of the world as no different from her search for answers that affected her school life. "I trust the process of events in our lives, of being open to things that make sense, to continually seek and know."

When asked if she had an artifact that best described her as a leader, one school principal shared a children's play she and her husband wrote years ago. It symbolized her devotion to her job as a school administrator, she said. She confided that her work often felt overwhelming, leaving very little time to explore creative pursuits. She lamented not writing and not playing the piano or guitar for years. Mostly, she did her job, spent time with her family, and then collapsed. In a low voice, she confessed that it's something she's worried and felt a little guilty about: "But there's always just so much to do."

As we continued to visit more and more school leaders, we were struck by the objects they collected and displayed. In a sense, these artifacts represented the lenses through which our leaders viewed their world. From personal artwork to favorite famous quotations, we discovered how leaders subconsciously surround themselves with symbols of their valued beliefs and enduring purposes as professionals.

USING ICONS AS METAPHORS FOR DESCRIBING PROFESSIONAL MISSION AND PURPOSE

An icon can be an image; a historical, spiritual, or imaginary person; an object; or a symbol. Like artifacts, icons are effective tools for eliciting creative ideas and understandings about our work, behaviors, attitudes, and beliefs. What's great about using icons is there's no end of objects and materials to use. Reflecting on icons involves divergent thinking that starts from a common focus and moves outward through a variety of perspectives. Working with icons in an organizational context is engaging, thought provoking, imaginative, and, best of all, fun!

During one of our professional development projects with principals and superintendents, we decided to use icons to help leaders identify their professional dispositions and performance competencies with the ISLLC standards developed by the Council of Chief State School Officers and adopted by many states for school administrator certification. When individuals and groups reflected on icons for each standard, leaders' responses were imaginative, informative, sometimes humorous, and insightful.

ISLLC Standard 1: The Vision of Learning

A school administrator is an educational leader who promotes the success of all students by facilitating the development, articulation, implementation, and stewardship of a vision of learning that is shared and supported by the school community.

Standard 1 Icon: A Telescope

This icon stimulated the following individual and group responses:

A leader creates vision by incorporating others' perspectives.

Visionary leaders look past the horizon.

Sometimes what we see, we don't always embrace.

Telescopes are like school leaders: good tools to inspire curiosity.

The telescope doesn't work if you don't remove the lens cover.

ISLLC Standard 2: The Culture of Teaching and Learning

A school administrator is an educational leader who promotes the success of all students by advocating, nurturing, and sustaining a school culture and instructional program conducive to student learning and staff professional growth.

Standard 2 Icon: A 1945 Report Card

This icon stimulated the following responses:

Hmm . . . some things haven't changed!

Is an A back then an A today?

Good leaders and report cards promote reflection and growth.

The report card reminds us to address the needs of all students.

Report cards show how students learn and how teachers teach.

ISLLC Standard 3: The Management of Learning

A school administrator is an educational leader who promotes the success of all students by ensuring management of the organization, operations, and resources for a safe, efficient, and effective learning environment.

Standard 3 Icon: A Thermostat

This icon stimulated the following responses:

The thermostat reminds us learning doesn't take place in a vacuum.

Setting the thermostat higher doesn't always get the climate we want.

In some schools there's a thermostat in every room. In other schools, there's only one in the entire building!

In our school district, the thermostat says 68 but it feels like 100!

ISLLC Standard 4: Relation to the Broader Community to Foster Learning

A school administrator is an educational leader who promotes the success of all students by collaborating with families and community members, responding to diverse community interests and needs, and mobilizing community resources.

Standard 4 Icon: Newspapers in Different Languages

This icon stimulated the following responses:

Newspapers are all too often black and white.

The different newspapers remind us there's more than one way to communicate.

If leaders inform people about their schools, support will follow.

Newspapers are like schools: informative, inviting, stimulating, engaging.

Not being able to read Japanese papers is like our kids in school who can't read English.

ISLLC Standard 5: Integrity, Fairness, and Ethics in Learning

A school administrator is an educational leader who promotes the success of all students by acting with integrity, with fairness, and in an ethical manner.

Standard 5 Icon: A Tarnished Mirror

This icon stimulated the following responses:

Sometimes the reflection I see is not what others see.

Leading ethically means examining our beliefs and our actions.

The mirror reminds us to practice what we preach.

At times when I reflect, it's not very clear.

The mirror is tarnished. In some ways, so are we.

ISLLC Standard 6: The Political, Social, Economic, Legal, and Cultural Context of Learning

Standard 6 Icon: A Three-Headed Statuette

This icon stimulated the following responses:

Are the heads all looking in the same direction?

The statuette has six eyes to help see the big picture.

The statuette's heads are like the constituencies we serve: too many.

Leadership requires multiple intelligences.

We continue to be surprised by school leaders' enthusiastic reactions to icons. Often, the discussions that arise in groups are alive with humorous anecdotes, insightful perspectives, and reflective viewpoints. Icons have a way of transforming complex ideas and issues into manageable and comprehensible concepts. They bridge the complex and abstract to uncomplicated and identifiable domains that leaders can relate to and understand.

Icons are effective tools for organizational assessment. They are nonthreatening and invite reflection that leads to creative expressions of how people feel, what they experience as members of an institution, where they'd like to see their organization headed, and what resources they need to get them there.

In summary, we've identified a number of tools in this chapter to assist leaders in the uses of metaphoric reflection within their organizations.

Our success with moving people and institutions to greater efficiency, increased motivation, and improved alignment between institutional goals and accomplishments has been attributed to many of the processes and strategies discussed in this book. Now it's your turn.

REFLECTION QUESTIONS AND ACTIVITIES

When was the last time you held a baby? If you can try to have that experience again, or if you can remember the last time you've had that experience, what comes to mind? Do the feelings or emotions persist even if the baby is 5? 15? 25? 45? 65? What changes? What if those beliefs and emotions were still core to us no matter what age the child? Would our schools look different? Would our practices change?

Leadership Assessment: Thinking Map Analysis

Create a **bubble map:** Draw a circle in the middle of a piece of paper. Write inside that circle "Instructional Leadership." Draw bubbles outside the center circle (Hyerle, 1996). In the bubbles, write the words or metaphors that come to mind when you think about instructional leadership.

Bubble Map

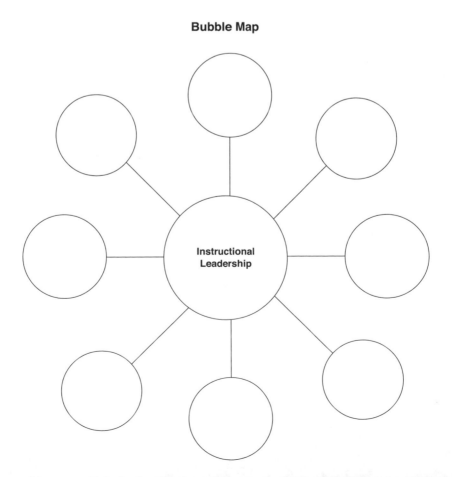

Instructional Leadership

Ask a colleague to do the same activity. Now compare and contrast your responses with a **double bubble map** (Hyerle, 1996).

Double Bubble Map

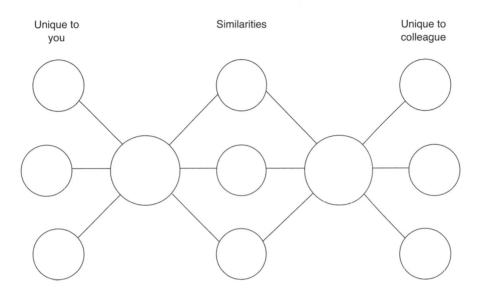

| Unique to you | Similarities | Unique to colleague |

What characteristics did you have in common? Identify characteristics that were different and unique to each of you. What did you learn?

Organizational Assessment: Metaphoric Analysis

We have focused on the use of metaphor to look at the issue of leadership in schools. It is also powerful to get feedback about how your staff feels about the learning and organizational environment. Present to your staff the following: "The working environment in my school is like. . . ." Get the responses and determine what your staff thinks about the current state of operations. What did you discover? In addition, you might prompt, "For my working environment to be successful or ideal it needs. . . ."

Finding
Common Ground

The door to novelty is always slightly ajar: many pass it by with barely a glance; some peek inside but choose not to enter . . . while a few, drawn by curiosity . . . venture in.

—Tom Robbins
Villa Incognita

Our primary aim for this book has been to dramatize the power of reflection by way of metaphor to motivate people and organizations toward more enlightened, inspired, and successful practice. We want to emphasize that no one metaphor can aptly describe who we are and how we act as leaders. The three archetypes in this book represent a new perspective about leadership that has not been addressed in the literature. The *Touchstone*, the *Advocate*, and the *Parent* provide conceptual lenses for understanding the relationship between core values, intrinsic beliefs, and leadership behaviors.

Looking back at our planning notes for the development of this book, we identified the following purposes for reframing by way of metaphor:

- Encourage people to think differently about themselves, their organization, and their relationship with the organization.
- Help people solve problems creatively and proactively.
- Identify a prevailing and outdated institutional myth and develop a new proactive story for your organization.
- Discourage the influence of resisters to change.
- Lead creative thinking and problem solving by example.
- Assess, reinforce, and perpetuate spiritual values within your organization.

LINK PERSONAL DEVELOPMENT WITH PROFESSIONAL AND ORGANIZATIONAL GROWTH

Exceptional leaders are risk takers and pioneers. They are not afraid to explore new avenues for developing their organizations as cohesive and vital learning communities. But exceptional leaders need new ideas, creative solutions, and inspired lessons from others to inform their practice. In that regard, we've tried to pique the interest of readers with proven examples from practitioners and novel activities we've used for professional development that are effective and doable. We've observed at many sessions how our training encourages and expands group dialogue, builds consensus, and moves people from old and pervasive patterns of dysfunctional behavior to inspired, proactive, and collective action.

Make no mistake, we are concerned that No Child Left Behind (NCLB) has all too often left administrators to wallow in the victim mythology we described earlier in the book. As one educator lamented, "our focus on educational reform with No Child Left Behind constantly raising the bar leaves us little time for such thought [about the spiritual values of leaders and organizations], maybe to our own peril." This is precisely the thinking that's frequently heard in central administrative and school principals' offices throughout America. It reflects an attitude of resignation, of accepting the status quo rather than seizing the opportunity to consider our purpose as educators and leaders to create new structures and responses to policies that challenge our professional standards, programs, and visions.

Tapping into the reflection activities we've provided can be useful especially for school leaders committed to guiding teachers beyond NCLB. By exposing the "stories" within their organizations as a first step to bringing their groups together, leaders can guide their organizations to develop effective strategies for improving both student and adult performance.

Our challenge, then, is for you to begin the process of developing your organization's "story." For instance, you might want to consider the "Lesson of the Geese" to help identify where you and the members of your leadership team are with respect to your organization's vision, goals, and beliefs.

LESSON OF THE GEESE

In the fall when you see geese heading south for the winter, flying along in the "V" formation, you might be interested to know what science discovered about why they fly that way. Scientists learned that as each bird flaps its wings, it creates uplift for the bird immediately following. By flying in a

"V" formation, the whole flock adds at least 71 percent greater flying range than the birds would have if each flew on its own.

Whenever a goose falls out of formation, it suddenly feels the drag and resistance of trying to go it alone and quickly gets back into formation to take advantage of the power of the flock. When the lead goose gets tired, he or she rotates back in the wing, and another takes over. The other geese honk from behind to encourage those up front to keep up their speed.

Finally, when a goose gets sick or is wounded and falls, two geese leave the formation and follow the injured one down to help protect him or her. They stay with the goose until he or she is either able to fly or is dead, and then they launch out with another formation to catch up with the group.

Considering this allegory through the lens of the leadership arche-types is one way to examine the relevance of the story to your organi-zation. The leader of the formation is the Touchstone. It knows how to navigate the currents of the winds, when to drop back and allow others to take the lead, all the while remaining steadfast in its vision for the flock. The Advocate represents distributive leadership whereby those geese that continue to "honk" from behind are committed to a cause beyond them-selves and to the success of the entire flock. The Parent, symbolizing the school or organization community, is represented by those geese that exhibit an ethic of care when supporting a goose unable to fly.

Finally, the compelling message of this book is our unwavering trust in the power of positive change and human ingenuity to enlighten indi-viduals and transform institutions toward creative and productive work. Reframing through metaphor is a powerful tool for organizational change that few leaders understand, much less use. Please use this book and our Web site (www.deconstructingthebox.org) as your gateway to novelty and to a new kind of leadership that has the potential to transform people and institutions.

Resource

ISLLC Standards

STANDARD 1

A school administrator is an educational leader who promotes the success of all students by facilitating the development, articulation, implementation, and stewardship of a vision of learning that is shared and supported by the school community.

Knowledge

The administrator has knowledge and understanding of:

- learning goals in a pluralistic society
- the principles of developing and implementing strategic plans
- systems theory
- information sources, data collection, and data analysis strategies
- effective communication
- effective consensus-building and negotiation skills

Dispositions

The administrator believes in, values, and is committed to:

- the educability of all
- a school vision of high standards of learning

NOTE: Reprinted with permission of the Council of Chief State School Officers (1996). *Interstate School Leaders Licensure Consortium (ISLLC) Standards for School Leaders*. Washington, DC: Author.

The ISLLC standards were developed by the Council of Chief State School Officers (CCSSO) and member states. Copies may be downloaded from the Council's Web site at www.ccsso.org.

- continuous school improvement
- the inclusion of all members of the school community
- ensuring that students have the knowledge, skills, and values needed to become successful adults
- a willingness to continuously examine one's own assumptions, beliefs, and practices
- doing the work required for high levels of personal and organization performance

STANDARD 2

A school administrator is an educational leader who promotes the success of all students by advocating, nurturing, and sustaining a school culture and instructional program conducive to student learning and staff professional growth.

Knowledge

The administrator has knowledge and understanding of:

- student growth and development
- applied learning theories
- applied motivational theories
- curriculum design, implementation, evaluation, and refinement of student learning as the fundamental purpose of schooling
- principles of effective instruction
- measurement, evaluation, and assessment strategies
- diversity and its meaning for educational programs
- adult learning and professional development models
- the change process for systems, organizations, and individuals
- the role of technology in promoting student learning and professional growth
- school cultures

Dispositions

The administrator believes in, values, and is committed to:

- student learning as the fundamental purpose of schooling
- the proposition that all students can learn
- the variety of ways in which students can learn
- lifelong learning for self and others
- professional development as an integral part of school improvement

- the benefits that diversity brings to the school community
- a safe and supportive learning environment
- preparing students to be contributing members of society

STANDARD 3

A school administrator is an educational leader who promotes the success of all students by ensuring management of the organization, operations, and resources for a safe, efficient, and effective learning environment.

Knowledge

The administrator has knowledge and understanding of:

- theories and models of organizations and the principles of organizational development
- operational procedures at the school and district level
- principles and issues relating to school safety and security
- human resources management and development
- principles and issues relating to fiscal operations of school management
- principles and issues relating to school facilities and use of space
- legal issues impacting school operations
- current technologies that support management functions

Dispositions

The administrator believes in, values, and is committed to:

- making management decisions to enhance learning and teaching
- taking risks to improve schools
- trusting people and their judgments
- accepting responsibility
- high-quality standards, expectations, and performances
- involving stakeholders in management processes
- a safe environment

STANDARD 4

A school administrator is an educational leader who promotes the success of all students by collaborating with families and community members, responding to diverse community interests and needs, and mobilizing community resources.

Knowledge

The administrator has knowledge and understanding of:

- emerging issues and trends that potentially impact the school community
- the conditions and dynamics of the diverse school community
- community resources
- community relations and marketing strategies and processes
- successful models of school, family, business, community, government, and higher education partnerships.

Dispositions

The administrator believes in, values, and is committed to:

- schools operating as an integral part of the larger community
- collaboration and communication with families
- involvement of families and other stakeholders in school decision-making processes
- the proposition that diversity enriches the school
- families as partners in the education of their children
- the proposition that families have the best interests of their children in mind
- resources of the family and community needing to be brought to bear on the education of students
- an informed public

STANDARD 5

A school administrator is an educational leader who promotes the success of all students by acting with integrity, fairness, and in an ethical manner.

Knowledge

The administrator has knowledge and understanding of:

- the purpose of education and the role of leadership in modern society
- various ethical frameworks and perspectives on ethics
- the values of the diverse school community

- professional codes of ethics
- the philosophy and history of education

Dispositions

The administrator believes in, values, and is committed to:

- the ideal of the common good
- the principles in the Bill of Rights
- the right of every student to a free, quality education
- bringing ethical principles to the decision-making process
- subordinating one's own interest to the good of the school community
- accepting the consequences for upholding one's principles and actions
- using the influence of one's office constructively and productively in the service of all students and their families
- development of a caring school community

STANDARD 6

A school administrator is an educational leader who promotes the success of all students by understanding, responding to, and influencing the larger political, social, economic, legal, and cultural context.

Knowledge

The administrator has knowledge and understanding of:

- principles of representative governance that undergird the system of American schools
- the role of public education in developing and renewing a democratic society and an economically productive nation
- the law as related to education and schooling
- the political, social, cultural, and economic systems and processes that impact schools
- models and strategies of change and conflict resolution as applied to the larger political, social, cultural, and economic contexts of schooling
- global issues and forces affecting teaching and learning
- the dynamics of policy development and advocacy under our democratic political system
- the importance of diversity and equity in a democratic society

Dispositions

The administrator believes in, values, and is committed to:

- education as a key to opportunity and social mobility
- recognizing a variety of ideas, values, and cultures
- the importance of a continuing dialogue with other decision makers affecting education
- actively participating in the political and policy-making context in the service of education
- using legal systems to protect student rights and improve student opportunities

References

Argyris, C. (1964). *Integrating the individual and the organization.* New York: John Wiley.

Baker, J. (2000). *Great green book of garden secrets.* Wixom, MI: American Master Products.

Beck, L., & Murphy, J. (1993). *Understanding the principalship: Metaphorical themes, 1920s to 1990s.* New York: Teachers College Press.

Bolman, L., & Deal, T. (2001). *Leading with soul: An uncommon journey of spirit.* San Francisco: Jossey-Bass.

Bolman, L., & Deal, T. (2003). *Reframing organizations: Artistry, choice, and leadership* (3rd ed.). San Francisco: Jossey-Bass.

Brubaker, D. L., & Coble, L. D. (2005). *The hidden leader: Leadership lessons on the potential within.* Thousand Oaks, CA: Corwin Press.

Campbell, J., & Moyers, B. (1988). *The power of myth.* New York: Doubleday.

Council of Chief State School Officers. (1996). *Interstate School Leaders Licensure Consortium (ISLLC) standards for school leaders.* Washington, DC: Author.

Denning, S. (2004). *Squirrel, Inc.* San Francisco: Jossey-Bass.

De Saint-Exupéry, A. (1943). *The little prince.* New York: Harcourt Brace.

Evans, R. (1996). *The human side of change: Reform, resistance and real-life problems of innovation.* San Francisco: Jossey-Bass.

Feinstein, D., & Krippner, S. (1988). *Using ritual, dreams and personal imagination to discover mythology.* Los Angeles: Jeremy Tarcher.

Freire, P. (1986). *The politics of education.* South Hadley, MA: Bergen & Garvey.

Fullan, M. (2001). *Leading in a culture of change.* San Francisco: Jossey-Bass.

Fullan, M. (2003). *The moral imperative of school leadership.* Thousand Oaks, CA: Corwin Press.

Gilligan, C. (1982). *In a different voice: Psychological theory and women's development.* Cambridge, MA: Harvard University Press.

Glickman, C. (2003). *Holding sacred ground.* Boston: Allyn & Bacon.

Goertz, J. (2000). Creativity: An essential component for effective leadership in today's schools. *The Roeper Review, 22,* 158–162.

Grahame, K. (1989). *Wind in the willows.* New York: New American Library-Dutton.

Hyerle, D. (1996). *Visual tools for constructing knowledge.* Alexandria, VA: Association for Supervision and Curriculum Development.

Jung, C. G. (1953). Archetypes of the collective unconscious. *Collected works* (Vol. 1). New York: Viking Press.

Kaiser, L. R. (2002). *Extended impact of spirituality.* Available online at www.spirit4greatness.com/admin/fileupload/articles/extended.pdf

Kreffing, L., & Frost, P. (1984). Untangling webs, surfing waves and wildcatting: A multiple metaphor perspective on managing organizational culture. In P. Frost et al. (Eds.), *Organizational culture* (pp. 155–168). Beverly Hills, CA: Sage.

Kolbenschlag, M. (1988). *Lost in the land of Oz.* San Francisco: Harper & Row.

Lakoff, G., & Johnson, M. (1980). *Metaphors we live by.* Chicago: University of Chicago Press.

L'Engle, M. (1962). *A wrinkle in time.* New York: Farrar, Straus & Giroux.

Morgan, G. (1986). *Images of organization.* Beverly Hills, CA: Sage.

Ortony, A. (1975). Why metaphors are necessary and not just nice. *Educational Theory, 25,* 45–53.

Owens, R., & Steinhoff, C. (1988, May). *An organizational cultural assessment inventory: A metaphorical analysis of organizational culture in educational settings.* Paper presented at the American Educational Research Association Meeting, New Orleans, Louisiana.

Reeves, D. (2002). *The daily disciplines of leadership.* San Francisco: Jossey-Bass.

Robbins, T. (2003). *Villa incognito.* New York: Bantam Books.

Sergiovanni, T. J. (1999). *The lifeworld of leadership: Creating culture, community, and public meaning in our schools.* San Francisco: Jossey-Bass.

Sousa, D. (2003). *The leadership brain.* San Francisco: Corwin Press.

Wilbur, K. (1979). *No boundary: Eastern and western approaches to personal growth.* Boston: New Science Library.

Wheatley, M. (1999). *Leadership and the new science.* San Francisco: Berrett-Koehler.

FURTHER READINGS

Adams, J. D. (1984). *Transforming work.* Alexandria, VA: Miles River Press.

Bagarozzi, D., & Anderson, S. (1989). *Personal, marital, and family myths.* New York: W. W. Norton.

Berg, P. O. (1983, August). *Corporate culture development: The strategic integration of identity, profile and image.* Paper presented at the meeting between the Nordic Schools of Business Administration, Copenhagen.

Bredeson, P. V. (1985). An analysis of metaphorical perspectives on school principals. *Educational Administration Quarterly, 21,* 29–59.

Brown, R. H. (1976). Social theory as metaphor: On the logic of discovery for the sciences of conduct. *Theory and Society, 3,* 169–197.

Bullough, R. V., Jr., & Stokes, D. K. (1994). Analyzing personal teaching metaphors in preservice teacher education as a means for encouraging professional development. *American Educational Research Journal, 32*(1), 220.

Comas-Diaz, L., & Greene, B. (Eds.). (1994). *Integrating ethnic and gender identities in psychotherapy.* New York: Guilford Press.

Dandridge, T. (1985). The life stages of a symbol: When symbols work and when they can't. In P. Frost, M. Louis, C. Lundberg, & J. Martin (Eds.), *Organizational culture* (pp. 141–153). Beverly Hills, CA: Sage.

Deal, T. (1985). The symbolism of effective schools. *The Elementary School Journal, 85*(5), 601–20.

Eisen, S., Nicoll, D., Owen, H., & Stephens, C. (1984). Facilitating organizational transformation: The uses of myth and ritual. In J. D. Adams (Ed.), *Transforming work* (pp. 209–224). Alexandria, VA: Miles River Press.

Furth, G. (1988). *The secret world of drawings.* New York: Sigo Press.

Gardner, H. (1983). *Frames of mind.* New York: Basic Books.

Goffman, E. (1974). *Frame analysis.* Cambridge, MA: Harvard University Press.

Greenfield, W. (1987). Moral imagination and interpersonal competence: Antecedents to instructional leadership. In W. Greenfield (Ed.), *Instructional leadership: Concepts, issues and controversies* (pp. 56–75). Norton, MA: Allyn & Bacon.

Grof, S. (1988). *Adventures of self-discovery.* Albany: SUNY Press.

Hall, E. (1983). *The silent language.* New York: Anchor Books.

Harris, R. W. (1987). *Gypsying after 40.* New York: W. W. Norton.

Jordan, J., Kaplan, G., Miller, J., Stiver, I., & Surrey, J. (1991). *Women's growth in connection: Writings from the Stone Center.* New York: Guilford Press.

Jung, C. G. (1964). *Man and his symbols.* Garden City, NY: Doubleday.

Lecioni, P. (2002). *The five dysfunctions of a team.* San Francisco: Jossey-Bass.

Meadows, O. (1967). The metaphors of order: Toward a taxonomy of organization theory. In L. Gross (Ed.), *Sociological theory: Inquiries and paradigms* (77–103). New York: Harper & Row.

Miller, J. B. (1991). The development of women's sense of self. In J. Jordan, G. Kaplan, J. Miller, I. Stiver, & J. Surrey (Eds.), *Women's growth in connection* (pp. 11–26). New York: Guilford Press.

Miller, S. I., & Frederickson, M. (1988). Uses of metaphor. A qualitative case study. *Qualitative Studies in Education, 1*(3), 263–264.

Olney, J. (1972). *Metaphors of self: The meaning of autobiography.* Princeton, NJ: Princeton University Press.

Pondy, L. R. (1982). The role of metaphors and myths in organizations and the facilitation of change. In L. R. Pondy, A. Wilkens, J. Andrews, & W. Ouchi (Eds.), *Organizational symbolism* (157–166). Greenwich, CT: JAI Press.

Spiegel, J. M. (1995). *The badger, the gypsy and everybody's mother: Exploring personal mythologies of women who principal schools.* Unpublished doctoral dissertation, University of Vermont.

Surrey, J. (1991). The self-in-relation: A theory of women's development. In J. Jordan, G. Kaplan, J. Miller, I. Stiver, & J. Surrey (Eds.), *Women's growth in connection* (pp. 51–66). New York: Guilford Press.

Vicere, A. A., & Filmer, R. M. (1997). *Leadership by design.* Cambridge, MA: Harvard Business School Press.

Von Oech, R. (2001). *Expect the unexpected.* New York: Free Press.

Wilkens, A. L. (1983). Organizational stories as symbols which control the organization. In L. R. Pondy, A. Wilkens, J. Andrews, & W. Ouchi (Eds.), *Organizational symbolism* (pp. 468–481). Greenwich, CT: JAI Press.

Index

CORWIN PRESS

The Corwin Press logo—a raven striding across an open book—represents the union of courage and learning. Corwin Press is committed to improving education for all learners by publishing books and other professional development resources for those serving the field of PreK–12 education. By providing practical, hands-on materials, Corwin Press continues to carry out the promise of its motto: **"Helping Educators Do Their Work Better."**